禅

ZEN
KOBUDO

ZEN

KOBUDO

Mysteries of Okinawan Weaponry
and Te

Mark Bishop

Charles E. Tuttle Company
Rutland, Vermont & Tokyo, Japan

Disclaimer

Please note that the author and publisher of this book are NOT RESPONSIBLE in any manner whatsoever for any injury that may result from practicing the techniques and/or following the instructions given within. Since the physical activities described herein may be too strenuous in nature for some readers to engage in safely, *it is essential that a physician be consulted prior to training.*

Published by the Charles E. Tuttle Company, Inc.
of Rutland, Vermont & Tokyo, Japan
with editorial offices at
2-6 Suido 1-chome, Bunkyo-ku, Tokyo 112

LCC Card No. 96-60293
ISBN 0-8048-2027-9

First edition, 1996
First reprint, 1997

Printed in Singapore

TO TRUE KNOWLEDGE
and all those
who have fought for peace, reason, and dignity
throughout the ages

Contents

MAPS

Introduction

"True knowledge is the road to everlasting peace," and I dedicate this work to that idea. In publishing this book, therefore, I do not intend to further the cause of the now-defunct, barbarous age of phantom chivalry and incessant warfare that was feudalism; an age when personal opinion was, after all, backed up by force of arms and when social distinctions were brutally imposed by an elite few on an oppressed majority. Rather, I propose to lay to rest all that the imagined romance of that autocratic era claims to represent, for under the blanket of its romance lies a sinister specter. Strange as it may seem, I, who have martial arts in my blood and backbone, believe that weapon practice should never be an excuse for any kind of violence, especially to control others, but a powerful means of helping to alleviate that scourge of history.

Thus, the information contained herein has been put forward as an important, modern-day cultural asset that can help to further individual development and creativity. The work is not intended to be a beautification of brutality, or a glorification of the mistakes of an ancient and evil epoch when the sword ruled supreme. These distorted negative images associated with the martial arts are a gory remnant of a withered time, the skeletal remains of a diseased nightmare that should be buried forever and left alone to decay in peace.

However, the positive aspects of martial arts—the concepts of nurturing, improving, and protecting oneself—that have brought civilization through the dark ages, are still very much alive in present-day Okinawa as a form of recreation, spiritual discipline, and health preservation. It is these aspects that I emphasize here, for I repeat that it is my sincere belief that the martial arts should not be used as a way of harming or dispatching one another. If used positively, the techniques of weapon training can become a catalyst of change for helping propel our rapidly changing world culture into a more open and enlightened future. Their abuse can be fatal, if not soul-destroying. I personally accept no responsibility whatsoever for the misuse of any weapon or technique listed herein; for this is no more the case than if I were a driving instructor whose former student had caused injury or death because he or she had abused the privileges of having a driver's license and acted irresponsibly. In today's world, in the wrong hands, there is no more lethal a weapon than the motor car—for it has surely taken over where the sword left off.

To many Westerners, the traditional cultures and traditional activities of the Orient seem to be wrapped in an impenetrable cloud of mystery. Philosophical attitudes, religious beliefs, and even the very nature of the languages themselves seem to be so far removed from reality as compared to those that one is closer to and more familiar with. Perhaps more than any other popularly practiced cultural entity, the martial arts that have recently come out of the East may appear to be the most mysterious of all. With their often cited "legendary pasts" and "many closely guarded secrets," the Okinawan martial arts, in all their aspects, could easily be looked upon to fit this description; but this need not necessarily be the case. In my earlier book, *Okinawan Karate: Teachers, Styles and Secret Techniques*, I attempted to demonstrate that, in reality, this part of Oriental culture is not any more unattainable or any less comprehensible to a person reared in the West than say, boxing or wrestling is to an individual brought up in the East.

What it boils down to is that no part of any particular culture need be unfathomable to any person from another cultural background; provided, that is, that the intricacies of the particular cultural entity are clearly laid out and passed on by written, or other appropriate means. My intention is to therefore unravel old mysteries, not to perpetuate them or to create new ones.

I hope that this book, like my previous book, will help to elucidate and thus further the understanding of the Okinawan martial arts that have of late become so popular throughout the world and have played such a major practical role in helping to understand what seemingly mysterious or different cultures and peoples are all about. This book will focus on the development of traditional hand-held weaponry and the teaching thereof, within the context of two distinct martial-art systems, Okinawan Te (or *Ti*) and Kobudo (or Kobu-jutsu)—Zen being the bonding integral factor between them. The two systems were formulated and are still taught on the southernmost islands of Japan, which, as a part of the Ryukyu Archipelago, now form the political subdivision of Okinawa Prefecture—

Okinawa being the main island of the group. Until 1879, the Ryukyu Islands, including most of the Northern Ryukyus, were a semi-independent, self-governing trading nation known and respected, far and wide, as the ancient and wealthy Kingdom of Ryukyu.

To present the material clearly, there are four distinct chapters. Chapter 1 sets the scene by grouping and listing the various weapons, while explaining exactly what Te and Kobudo are. It then follows through by introducing the basic historical social structure of Okinawa, the various religious practices and how they relate to Zen, with commentary on weapon dances as they correspond to the martial arts. The last topic of this chapter deals with the so-called metaphysical aspects of Zen and the meditative process, with correct posture and breathing. Chapter 2 traces the history of weapon development, starting with crude, Stone Age tools, through a mythical time, to feudalism, and finishes in the Golden Age of Trade, when finely honed swords, with other valuable bladed weapons, were traded at high prices worldwide. The ancient history of stylized martial arts, as they affected the surrounding regions as well as the associated philosophies, is also examined very thoroughly in this chapter; as is the important role of Zen, with its relationship to religious schools of thought such as Buddhism and Daoism.

Chapters 3 and 4 deal more with the introduction of Te and Kobudo to Okinawa, as well as looking at Zen from this angle, giving a more human face to weapon-system development by describing the characters who have affected it. In Chapter 3 the undiscovered tap roots of Te are researched closely and brought to the surface to reveal some intriguing, previously undisclosed, hidden secrets. Then the preservation of Te, through dance, drama, and seemingly intelligent determination, is dealt with, paralleling the arrival of Kobudo from China. The two systems' subsequent transformation into the modern era as important living cultural treasures, is also dealt with. Chapter 4 gives details of the six major commercial postwar styles, with information on their respective unique specialties, founders, and/or teachers. Two of these styles, Motobu-ryu and Bugeikan, are Te oriented, while the remaining four, Uhuchiku Kobudo, Ryukyu Kobudo, Honshin-ryu, and Matayoshi Kobudo, are definitively Kobudo styles. Their common denominator is seen as the combined anatomical, physiological, and metaphysical process of Zen—enlightenment.

Because language is the reflection of a people, as are their martial arts, many relevant Japanese and Okinawan words (along with some of Chinese and Sanskrit origin) have been purposefully introduced to the text. As this work is an in-depth study of Okinawan martial arts weapons and Zen, it is hoped that the inclusion of these important words will be appreciated for their worth and that the reader's vocabulary and understanding will be enriched by them. To aid in the appreciation of these words, a comprehensive Glossary-Index has been included. Likewise, a Bibliography has been included to help further the reader's knowledge on the subject matter involved.

Contrary to the golden rule of "love thy neighbor as thyself," the despising of one's neighbors, due to ignorance of their ways or beliefs, has been a major source of friction between peoples for thousands of years, which has led to endless wars, with the compounded need to develop greater and more sophisticated weapons with which to kill and maim the "other" people. It is an interesting quirk of history therefore that knowing more about the antiquated weapons and weapon systems of a bygone age, in a once far-off, forgotten land, may help to bring about a better understanding of differing cultures that hopefully will be another step along the peaceful way we all so long to tread.

—THE AUTHOR

Naha, Okinawa

1

Outline of Weapons
and Culture

Weapons, as will be seen, have been used on Okinawa, as in most cultures, since before the dawn of history, when primitive Stone Age implements were employed to murder people instead of for hunting animals. The techniques for these have been lost, but what is unique about the Okinawan heritage is that the later introduced refined and stylized weapons systems and strategies have been handed down for over a thousand years, almost intact with few alterations, to the present generations.

The weapons used in Te and Kobudo range in shape and substance from the deadly macabre to the seemingly ineffective; from the swift and silent projectile bow and arrow to the innocent-looking wooden agricultural flail and from the sinister curved sword to the effeminate, yet effective (in trained hands), bamboo and silk fan. In all, fifty hand-held weapons have been recorded, which are generally sorted into twenty-one different types, namely: bow and arrow; sword; glaive (sometimes called a halberd); hand spear; sharp implement with shield; sickle; hoe; three-pronged truncheon; weight and chain; knuckle-duster; metal rod; staff; stick; oar; flail; right-angle handle truncheon; umbrella; fan; hairpin; other accessories (which includes tobacco pipes, musical plectrums, and dried beans); and firearms. Although these types of weapons have never been systematically categorized in writing before, I thought it appropriate to break with convention and list them in some kind of ordered classification for inclusion in the following index and for their further detailed study.

Before a final decision was made on what categories to use, several loosely defined concepts were carefully looked at. These included the more obviously popular, dual designation of "agricultural-based weapons" as opposed to "non-agricultural-based weapons" and the contrasting of "Te-based weapons" to "Chinese-based Kobudo weapons." However, although these general groupings are frequently resorted to verbally by many Kobudo and Te teachers on Okinawa, they are neither clear-cut nor comprehensive enough for use in this book. In this respect, there is no real distinct difference between what is, or is not, an agricultural-based weapon—the definition of such being purely subjective. No one can define with authority what constitutes a Te-based weapon, or a Chinese-based Kobudo one either; for although the weapon may be the same, its techniques during practice will be quite different in the two systems.

Historically speaking, for example, Te was concerned mostly with metal-bladed weaponry, however the blunt wooden oar has remained a part of the Te repertoire since time immemorial, adapting of late Kobudo techniques and forms as well. Therefore, after much careful deliberation, a sensible, non-partisan weapon classification, based more on simple convenience rather than anything else, was decided upon. This categorizes them as either "metal," "wooden," or "other weapons." The first category is further divided into two subdivisions each namely: "bladed metal weapons," which include bow and arrow, sword, knife, glaive, hand spear, and sickle, and "non-bladed metal weapons" such as the three-pronged truncheon with its variations and the knuckle-duster. "Wooden weapons" include the staff, flail, and right-angle handle truncheon, whereas "other weapons" are the less familiar implements or weapons, such as the paper umbrella, fan, and the Okinawan hairpin, in addition to the other accessories and firearms mentioned earlier.

However, these groupings are not clear-cut either, because few of the weapons are actually all wood or all metal, most being composed, to varying extents, of both materials. Whereas the three-pronged truncheon is made entirely of iron, steel, or bronze, the sword, with its all-steel blade, will have a partly wooden hilt, while the glaive has a long, wooden handle with a metal cutting, or slicing, edge on the end. In this way, the bow and arrow, which is mostly a wooden weapon, is listed in the "bladed metal weapons" category, because it has a metal cutting edge at its lethal end in the form of the arrowhead.

What is meant by "non-bladed metal weapons" is any weapon without a cutting, slicing, or stabbing edge for piercing human flesh. The wooden weapons usually contain no metal at all, whereas those listed under "other weapons," may be constructed of either wood or metal, or be composite. The latter have been listed as such, more for their general unfamiliarity, or strangeness, rather than for anything else. All the recorded weapons, except for those listed under the titles bow and arrow, other accessories, and firearms, are still taught as a part of the Te or Kobudo systems, in a safe manner, by highly skilled and responsible masters at their respective schools.

List of Okinawan Weaponry

Metal Weapons (Bladed)

WEAPON NAME	TYPES	DESCRIPTION
1. Bow and arrow	*yumi-ya, oyumi*	large bow, or longbow
	koyumi	short bow
	ishi-yumi	crossbow
2. Sword	*katana*	single-edged curved sword
	ryoba katana	double-edged straight sword
	tanto, kogatana	short sword, or knife
	yamanaji, *yamakatana*	(*lit.,* mountain sword) a broad-bladed, single-edged sword
3. Glaive	*naginata*	Japanese-type glaive
	bisento	Chinese-type glaive
4. Hand spear	*yari, hoko*	spear
	puku	hunting spear
	tuja	three-pronged fishing spear
5. Sharp implement and shield	*tinbe, tinbei*	short-handled spear-like weapon or long machete, used in conjunction with a leather shield or straw hat
6. Sickle	*kama, nichogama, nicho kama, mamori kama, irana*	sickle, usually used in pairs
	kusarigama	two sickles connected by a length of chain
	rokushaku kama	180-cm (6-*shaku*) staff surmounted by a large sickle blade
	toyei nobori kama,	170-cm pole sur-

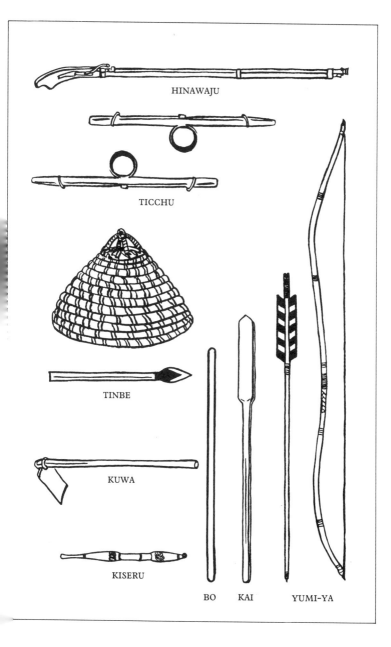

HINAWAJU

TICCHU

TINBE

KUWA

KISERU

BO   KAI   YUMI-YA

WEAPON NAME	TYPES	DESCRIPTION
	nata	mounted by a hatchet-shaped iron blade
7. Hoe	*kuwa, kue*	broad-bladed, mattock-like agricultural hoe

Metal Weapons (non-bladed)

8. Three-pronged truncheon	*sai*	metal truncheon with three prongs, one straight (about 40 cm in length); usually used in pairs
	manji no sai	variation of the *sai*, with one prong, or flange, turned up
	nuntei, nunti	212-cm (7-*shaku*) staff, with a *manji no sai*-like implement affixed to one end
9. Weight and chain	*suruchin*	long chain, weighted at both ends, some-times made of rope
	gekiguan	stick (about 102 cm in length) with a weighted chain or rope attached to one end
10. Knuckle-duster	*tekko*	iron (or wood) knuckle-duster, usually used in pairs
11. Metal rod (to hold in the hand)	*ticchu, tecchu, techu*	short, tapered, metal (or wooden) rod (about 20 to 30 cm in length) with a swivel ring attached at the center

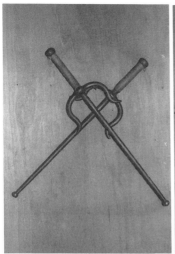

Sai.

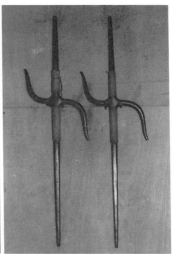

Manji no sai.

Kama.

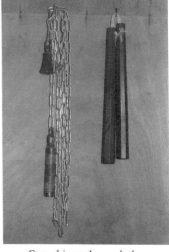

Suruchin and *nunchaku.*

Wooden Weapons

WEAPON NAME	TYPES	DESCRIPTION
12. Staff	*rokushaku bo, kon, kun, bo*	180-cm (6-*shaku*) staff
	hasshaku bo	240-cm (8-*shaku*) staff
	kyushaku bo	270-cm (9-*shaku*) staff
13. Stick	*jo, tsue, sutiku, sanjaku bo, yonshaku bo*	90- to 120-cm stick
	goshaku bo	150-cm (5-*shaku*) stick
	tankon	short stick (about 60 cm in length) for single-handed use
	take no bo	bamboo stick or cane
	gusan, gusan jo	heavy, ovoid cross-sectioned stick (about 102 cm in length)
	tanbo, nijo tanbo	pair of short, stubby sticks
14. Oar	*kai, ieku, eku, ueku*	long, paddle-like oar
15. Flail	*nunchaku, nunchiku, nunchakukun, renchaku, sosetsu kun, nuchiku*	flail-like weapon consisting of two rods joined by a length of rope or chain
	sanbon nunchaku, sanchaku kun, sansetsu kun	triple-sectioned, flail-like weapon, the rods of which are joined by short lengths of rope or chain
	dajio	Two wooden rods (about 15 cm in length) joined by a long length of rope
	uchi bo, renkuwan	long-handled, flail-like weapon with the two

Tekko.

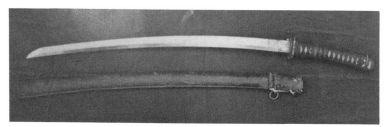

Katana.

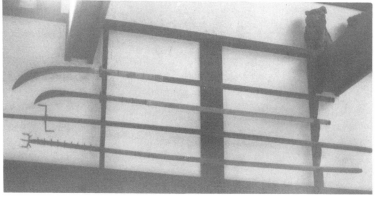

Glaives and spears.

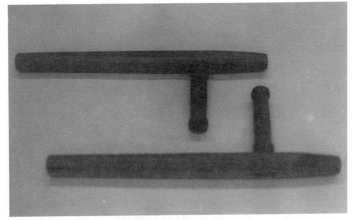

Tonfa.

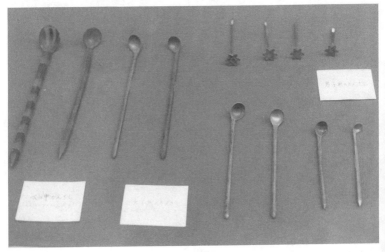

Hairpins.

WEAPON NAME	TYPES	DESCRIPTION
		rods (of unequal length) joined by a short length of rope
	sansetsu kun	Three rods (each about 65 cm in length) joined by two short lengths of chain
16. Right-angle handle trunchcon	*tonfa, tunfa, tuifa, toifua, tonkua, taofua, tonfua, tunkua, tuiha*	wooden rod (about 40 cm in length) with a handle fixed at a right angle near one end; usually used in pairs

Other Weapons

17. Umbrella	*kasa*	paper-and-bamboo umbrella or sunshade
18. Fan	*ogi*	paper or cloth fan carried by the Okinawan nobility
19. Hairpin	*kanzashi*	hairpin used by males and females to fasten the topknot in place
20. Other accessories	*kiseru*	tobacco pipe
	chimi	plectrum for musical instruments
	mame	dried bean (as a throwing weapon)
21. Firearms *(kaki)*	*kenju*	flintlock pistol
	hinawaju	musket

What Is Kobudo and Te?

The term *Kobudo* literally means "old martial arts." In actuality, it generally refers to practice and training with hand-held weaponry; more often than not of the non-bladed and so-called "agricultural-tool-based" varieties, but also the sword, glaive, or hand spear—the latter three being historically more associated with Te. On Okinawa, Chinese-based Kobudo weaponry has often been taught alongside, but as a separate art form from, the popular weaponless fighting systems labeled collectively as Karate (*lit.*, empty hands), which were formerly called Tode (or *Tuti*). This latter term, Tode, was derived from two words of one Chinese character each, namely *to* meaning China and *te* meaning hand (or hands), but in this case standing for fighting arts. The literal translation of Tode is therefore simply "Chinese Boxing." Going by close observation of their forms, among other things, the long stances, flat/anchored footwork and more straight-line arm movements of both Chinese-based Kobudo and Karate clearly show them to have common roots. There is no doubt that these roots reach back to China and, for the most part, the modern-day styles are based on Chinese Shaolin-derived forms that were introduced to Okinawa from the Fuzhou area as personal fighting arts, or weapon dances, within the last two hundred years.

On the other hand, Te and its weaponry systems clearly predates the advent of Chinese-derived Kobudo on Okinawa by several hundred years and, unlike the later Kobudo, it contains a multiplicity of empty-hand techniques. Although most of the weapons seen in Chinese-based Kobudo practice have more recently been adapted to Te training and incorporated into the system, the main weapons associated with Te have always been the sword, glaive, and hand spear. The tendency towards "soft," circular movements in Te are obviously dissimilar to the largely "hard," angular movements of Chinese-based Kobudo, demonstrating a quite different origin—an origin that is more open to conjecture. It is known however that, apart from ceremonial weapons,

Bo versus *sai:* Ryukyu Kobudo training at the Shinbukan.

which were usually of Chinese origin or design, the main bladed weapons used in Te practice were and still are of the manner and similar in use to those found in old Japan. The overall fluidity and sometimes springy footwork of Te, plus the hand techniques incorporating much grappling, *atemi* (vital-point striking), and the use of therapeutic pressure points, strongly suggest that it is a distant cousin of such Japanese martial arts as Ken-jutsu and Ju-jutsu, from which the modern sport-oriented, stylized fighting arts, like Kendo and Judo, have been developed in the twentieth century.

If Te shares a common source with, or is an offshoot of, ancient Japanese martial art methods, it would reflect and correspond to the general trend in Okinawan culture, from language and mannerisms to drama and dance, which all have their tap roots in ancient Japan (i.e., Yamato), but which have a distinct flavor of their own. Another interesting point to mention here about Te is that it has always been a weapon-oriented martial art, although the term literally means "hand" or "hands." Before the Kingdom of Ryukyu was effectively demilitarized by the invading Satsuma clan in 1609, the highly developed range of grappling techniques (with striking and pressure points) that Te boasts were used to get hold of another weapon by disarming an opponent, should one have been foolish, or unlucky, enough to have lost one's weapon on the battlefield. Therapeutic techniques were meant for aiding wounded comrades, but were also used to treat civilians.

After the Satsuma invasion, the techniques were developed more for personal self-defense and healing in general, while weapon practice was passed on with caution from teacher to student, or father to son, under the scrutinizing eyes of the ever-watchful *metsuke* (informers). It is wrong though to look at Te weapon and grappling (or empty-hand) techniques as being separate areas from each other. They are actually so interlinked that the advanced forms of the empty-hand Te techniques correspond exactly to the movements used when a weapon is being wielded; to such a degree in fact that a practitioner who has trained in only empty-hand techniques can easily adapt to using weapons and vice versa.

Although it can and has been argued that Te techniques and the associated bladed weapons are indigenous to Okinawa, it does seem more than likely that they were in fact originally introduced to the Ryukyu Islands from the Japanese mainland, probably long before the seventeenth and possibly as early as the seventh century A.D. One thing

Sea of Japan and East China Sea Area

is certain though; after the invasion of the Kingdom of Ryukyu by the Satsuma clan, no physical fighting form of any kind was used or organized in any way by Okinawans to attempt to overthrow the new overlords. Such contemplation to the contrary by various authors of late is a slight to an erudite and intelligent people whose ancestors, at that time, had evolved a sophisticated and well-organized society based on Confucian and feudal ideology. Such hearsay is speculation, without the glimmer of factual evidence, that ignores the mature diplomacy and statesmanship prevalent in Okinawa at that time; a trait that remains strongly embedded in all aspects of life to this day, including martial arts training. This wisdom of the ages is known to us as "turning the other cheek." Survival under the yoke of Satsuma was seen as political maneuvering, not armed rebellion.

After 1609, any martial arts or fighting systems that were practiced in, developed, or introduced to the Ryukyu Islands were done so by individuals or families for recreation, spiritual development, or personal self-defense. Although it is often stated otherwise, it should also be clarified that Okinawan peasants did not develop weapons from their agricultural tools for an imagined uprising; but that is not to say of course that implement-cum-weapons have not been used in Kobudo (or Te) practice. This seeming riddle is easily explained by sifting through the historical facts, which show that all the so-called "agricultural-based weapons" nowadays taught as part of Okinawan Kobudo, in the past as well as in the present, have their counterparts in China. In fact, similar agricultural-based weapons and Chinese Shaolin-based systems, corresponding to the Chinese-based Kobudo styles found in Okinawa, can be observed in parts of Southeast Asia. The majority of these styles were introduced there in the late nineteenth or early twentieth century by immigrants from China—some of whom had fled the aftermath of the Boxer Rebellion of 1900.

Social Structure of Okinawa

Virtually until 1879 and the complete takeover of the Ryukyuan government by the central Japanese authorities, the social structure of the Kingdom of Ryukyu was, by all definitions, undemocratic, being controlled by a set of rules and regulations that severely restricted the freedoms of both commoners and *shizoku* (aristocrats) alike. Peasants remained little more than serfs; they were virtually tied to the land—unless they were lucky enough to live in fishing communities with the freedom of the sea on their doorsteps; they were generally forbidden to learn how to read, write, or practice martial arts; they walked barefoot, even during the summer monsoon or cold winter months, and were utterly poverty-stricken, only being allowed to live in tiny thatched cottages. At the other end of the social scale, the comparatively wealthy *shizoku*, in their comfortable straw sandals and spacious castles, or (later) tiled villas in the capital at Shuri, had become slotted into their own rigid social structure, with the king and his family at the top, followed by nine lower grades of Anji, Uekata, Pechin, Satunushi Pechin, Chikudun Pechin, Satunushi, Waka Satunushi, Chikudun, and Chikudun Zashiki.

In all aspects of life, except for religious matters and childbirth, the male was usually dominant. It was not until 1724 that some restrictions on the *shizoku* (who had been centralized at Shuri) were lifted, unleashing a virtual tidal wave of immigration into the countryside; allowing the refined Shuri culture of these new pioneers to be observed throughout the islands by the still illiterate and subjugated country folk. The *shizoku* who became pioneers had no other practical use for their martial arts than to impress the villagers by putting on the occasional show at village or island festivals. The remnants of these martial art-based dances and plays can still be observed in various festivals today throughout the islands, with the participants dressed in mock samurai garb. They are a living peace memorial to a warring martial past.

Religious Practices and Zen

The ill-defined native Ryukyuan religious practices, sometimes conveniently lumped together and called *Ukami*, have unfortunately been haphazardly classified as a form of Animism; often because they have been misunderstood by non-Okinawan writers. One reason for this misrepresentation is that some of the devotees have stated to interviewers a belief in the concept that everything in nature has an innate spirit which they call *kami*; but *kami* also means gods, God, or an ancestral spirit—so what does this mean? A self-acclaimed devotee is a *kaminchu*, a god-like person, a saint or sensitive who has *kami* within them.

Looking at the religious practices of the population of Okinawa Prefecture in general, it is not difficult to observe that several religious beliefs have been formulated into a rather mixed-up collection of rituals and thought patterns with many and varied facets, shared between various family groups and individuals—each having his or her own peculiar interpretation of the religious beliefs! There is (again mislabeled) "Nature Worship" in sacred groves, which is probably influenced by the same ancient religion as Japanese Shinto, for some of the formal priestesses have, as a mark of their ceremonial office, similar comma-shaped jade stones (*magatama*) as the priestesses of old Japan; such as those that still make up part of the sacred imperial crown jewels of the Japanese Emperor. Some Shinto purification, dedication, and marital rites are popular in the urban areas of Okinawa, like Naha City. *Hi no kami*, the God of Fire, suggests Persian Zoroastrian influence and can be observed in even the most up-to-date, hi-tech kitchens.

Confucianism was transplanted from China and is seen in the form of filial piety shown toward parents and reverence for ancestors, formally expressed regularly at the family household altar, but rarely at a Confucian temple. Japanese-style Buddhism has its foothold in some beliefs and ceremonies (especially funeral rites), along with branches of Japanese temple foundations (including Zen Buddhist orders), new and old. Historical traces of Christianity, often disguised as Buddhism, as in Kannon temples (Guanyin in Chinese; the Goddess of Mercy or Compas-

Worship at a sacred grove.

A statuette of Kannon (Guanyin) at Tama- gusuku Castle.

sion—a representation of Mary in Buddhist guise), are evi- dent because the Ryukyu Islands were used as a secret base for Christian missionary activity during the centuries that Christianity and its teachings were forbidden in Japan proper. Nowadays most large international Christian groups have churches or offices somewhere on the Okinawan is- lands.

The teachers of some styles of martial arts may include theological training taken from various Buddhist sects, but there is no evidence that such theology was taught con- sciously as part of martial art training until the latter half of this century. In Okinawa Prefecture, any attempt to amalgamate organized religion with the martial arts would appear to be an essentially modern innovation. Unlike in several areas of China, there has never been a Shaolin Temple foundation in the Ryukyu Islands. On the whole, most styles do not include religious ceremonies, or theology, as part of the curriculum, whatever the religious beliefs of the head teacher may be. Basically, this is due to socioeconomic factors, in that any hint of religious indoctrination would, more likely than not, be detrimental to new student enrollment or would lead to the loss of a teacher's student body altogether. It could also be due to the male belief that religious matters are essentially a female preoccupation—religion being one of the few forms of legitimate protection and authority afforded to women until unbiased voting rights were introduced by the post-WWII American administration and reaffirmed after reversion to Japan in 1972.

All said and done, few Okinawans have a strict belief in just one particular religious order—many practice no religion at all, but the majority observe traditional religious customs of their choice. *Zazen* (sitting or kneeling meditation), *kokyuho* (breathing exercises), and other mind/spirit training methods, usually associated with Zen (Chan in Chinese, Dhyana in Sanskrit) teachings are an essential, if not integral, part of the Te and Kobudo styles. But one must be careful not to confuse the nonpartisan spiritual training of Zen with the organized religious practices of Zen Buddhism, which grew up in China and Japan around Zen teachings and meditation. In this context then, Zen-type meditative practices, not Zen Buddhism, play a major role in all Okinawan martial arts training—albeit an unwritten one.

Zen (i.e., meditation), as the Way (*Do* or *Dao*), a path to enlightenment or truth in the form of spiritual freedom, through various exercises as found in martial arts training, without the restrictive dogmas of religion, is a real but hidden concept in nearly every type of traditional Japanese (and Okinawan) training, from tea ceremony and flower arranging to archery and bonsai. All Japanese lifestyles are thus, to a greater or lesser extent, affected from cradle to grave by Zen. The point is that, the popular sixth-century teacher and folk celebrity, Daruma (Bodhidharma; or Damo, in Chinese), who transported his brand of martial art, therapy, and humor from southern India to China and who was the progenitor of the philosophical, anatomical, and physiological training passed on under the term Zen, is such a cult figure in Japanese and Okinawan life that his ideals are firmly embedded and finely interwoven within the very fabric of society today. His character, face, and thought patterns turn up everywhere from election campaigns to the realms of saké drinking and children's toys. Daruma, the man, the father figure, and Zen, his teachings, are the hidden strength that makes Japan, Okinawa, and their martial arts tick.

The religion of Zen Buddhism, which was founded long after Daruma's death, was an evangelical revival of older forms of Buddhism, and was popularized in Japan centuries later by Eisai, or Yosai, (1141–1215), who founded the Shofuku-ji and Jufuku-ji temples, which developed into the Rinzai sect. Then there was Dogen (1200–53) who founded the Eihei-ji temple in 1255, which became the Soto sect. These were followed by several others, including Bennen (1202–80) and Rankei Doryu (1213–78). The older forms of Buddhism that had officially started to take root in Japan in the mid-sixth century A.D., and were later popularized under the statesman Shotoku Taishi at Asuka near Nara in the late sixth and early seventh centuries, had been an import from Korea and China and were influenced by other religious teachings, including Zoroastrianism and Christianity from Persia. This organized religion, along with stylized martial arts and Zen, probably entered the Ryukyu Islands with the first missionaries from Nara in the early seventh century. These missionaries, as will be seen in the next chapter, were to play a major role in bringing civilization to the Ryukyu Islands.

However, Zen Buddhism, as a formal religion on Okinawa, is first recorded to have appeared when in the late thirteenth century a shipwrecked Japanese priest, Zenkan, constructed a small church in the old capital at Urasoe, near Shuri. By the early fifteenth century, several Buddhist temples had been established in the Ryukyu Islands, mostly in the capital at Shuri. These included the Zen Buddhist foundation Tenryu-ji, which had its headquarters in Kyoto (the then-capital of Japan) and was heavily involved in trade. Nowadays, as in the past, none of the schools that teach Te and Kobudo are directly affiliated to any of the Buddhist temples in Okinawa Prefecture, however, one school happens to be run by a teacher who is a Buddhist priest. His role, though, would be the equivalent of the local priest being coach of a rural sports team.

It is for financial reasons that the majority of Te and Kobudo schools are situated in populous areas, but this does not necessarily mean that commercialization is rampant—or even detrimental to martial arts. Most head teachers are barely able to pay the mortgages or rental on their concrete or wooden dojos. If fame and fortune are to be made, it is in having the status symbol of several branch schools overseas and the student numbers to go with them. Among most Te and Kobudo teachers, sincere dedication to their art is definitely the rule of the day. Monetary rewards would seem to be minimal.

Weapons Dances and Martial Arts

In compiling the information for this book, I have purposely avoided covering weapon dances in any depth, because these are considered to be a cultural entity unto themselves. However, I felt it necessary to include some information on them. Where to draw the line between weapon forms taught or practiced as martial arts and those performed as weapon dances proved not to be such a problem as I had initially supposed; even though the eighteenth-century choreography of the ancient classical (or court) dances, dramas, and operas are a time capsule of Te, plus the kata(s)—stylized dynamic forms—and the techniques of Kobudo often correspond exactly to the weapon dances observed at traditional village festivals. When therefore is a martial art not a martial art? Or, to put things into context, when is weapon practice not weapon practice, and just a weapon dance? The answer must be simply, when weapon katas are performed to music merely for entertainment or as an artistic, outwardly expressive dance.

The aim of weapon practice, as differentiated from performing weapon dances, should not be to just look good, but to promote health, self-development, and mental and spiritual awareness. Weapon practice is Zen in motion, with all its simplicity and all its complexity. Te and Kobudo are supposed to be, like weapon dances, aesthetically beautiful of course, but let it not be forgotten by the reader that, like the proverbial thorn of the English rose, these fighting systems can also have sinister aspects, concealed by their outward gracefulness. Martial arts were not developed merely by well-meaning, contemplative, saintly monks for improving or nurturing health, or as a means of self-protection by disarming adversaries. They were also developed with deadly intentions: to hurt, terrorize, and destroy human beings in the most effective ways possible.

In adept or unskilled hands alike, the weapons, whether learned as a dance or incorporated into martial art systems, are still in this modern age able to perform perverse, sordid, and grisly tasks when the psychology of the user is wrong or evil. I therefore reiterate my trust that the reader will accept the knowledge divulged within this work for the sake of knowledge and will not abuse the trust that goes with attaining it. An eternal truth to be reckoned with here is, as Daruma would most assuredly have agreed, "Those who live by the sword shall die by the sword." For are we not all bound by the karmic laws of cause and effect, to reap that which we have sown—be it evil, or be it good; be it death, or be it life?

Traditional Okinawan weapons dance.

Zen and Body Dynamics

What therefore is this mysterious Zen and how can one attain "enlightenment" through training in the martial arts? To answer this frequently asked question, it is first necessary to point out that the practice of Zen, or meditation, is not really mysterious at all; no more than is shoveling sand with a good clean shovel. However, it often appears to be so because of the erroneous association of Daruma's Zen with Zen Buddhism and other religious orders that falsely profess to follow his teachings. These religious bodies would have their initiates believe that self-discovery, or enlightenment, is a purely mental exercise done while one is sitting meditating or praying for hours on end, pointlessly contemplating one's own navel—the priest being the untouchable, perfect, all-knowing master dangling the keys, like carrots before a donkey, in front of the devotees' eyes while professing to have the power and esoteric knowledge to open the doors of the believers' souls for them.

Nothing could be further from the truth, for we all possess our own keys of life. The key factor being that, unless one first works to open up the body, the mind has nothing to follow. Sitting around doing nothing is only a small part of the meditative process towards discovering emptiness and is only a part of it as long as the "doing nothing" is a long-term constructive process. The path to enlightenment, the Way, is through sheer hard work on both a physical and an intellectual level, not by intellectualizing about sheer hard work on a physical and intellectual level and doing nothing about it. Spiritual freedom comes through doing the right things, not by just thinking about doing the right things. Thus, primarily, physical training is the first important step towards leading a fulfilling life, and this means correct physical training in the proper body dynamics that conform to the natural capacities of the human physique, exercises that help set the body free.

It is this training that is essential to discovering, getting in touch with, or becoming one with one's higher self or the angelic side of one's subconscious. Intellectual thought patterns should be interlinked with the proper physical training, so that the finer spiritual matter of the soul will permeate the coarser physical matter throughout one's person. For this to happen there must be emptiness of ego within— one must be free of stress. Training procedures that nurture rather than punish the body should be adhered to. Thus a martial arts practitioner should begin his or her workout with a series of preparatory warming-up exercises to loosen up, elongate, and tone the soft tissues. Such exercises should be performed in coordination with breathing, exhaling as a rule through the mouth when stretching out, blocking, punching, kicking, etc. In this way the whole body, especially the joints, will become more flexible. Emphasis should be placed on the hip joints and spine. Actually, before beginning training, the body and mind are usually quite tense, so through the preparatory exercises the practitioner is releasing the stress of the day and starting to induce a relaxed state. The more tonified the body and relaxed or at ease the mind become, the more active the workout can be without damaging the body. Eventually the trainee will be able to become "hard" or "soft" at will and have mastery over regulating body control.

The goal here is to put the meditative process into martial arts movements (whether they be gentle, as in Te and Taijiquan, or robust, like those of Chinese-based Kobudo and Karate), eventually incorporating them into one's everyday life. Keeping the former concepts in mind and endeavoring to put them into practice, the beginner must remember to "drop" the shoulders while performing basic movements, like simple kata, which help develop coordination of the left and right limbs. The next stage is to start directing the strength out from the hips during training, especially from the abdominal area. Then, one should learn how to breathe deeply by drawing air into the lungs by using the lower abdominal muscles—but that is not to say that breathing with the chest should be abandoned. In the next step, one has to practice by moving from the feet. That is to say within reason, that all movements should start in the feet and be directed by the waist, just as young children do naturally. The breath should follow and eventually one will feel as if one is "breathing with the soles of the feet." The intrinsic energy, or *ki,* will follow suit and flow freely throughout the body to be directed anywhere by the mind or focused on a single point.

After a good workout along these lines, the trainee will be well prepared for sitting meditation; going from action to inaction, from an active external state where the spirit (or subconscious) is passive to a passive internal state where the spirit is active. Whatever position for sitting meditation is adopted it must be comfortable. Thus, if kneeling or sitting cross-legged is not feasible, sitting on a chair is recommended. However, the appropriate training to help the trainee to eventually be able to sit at ease in any meditative position should be taught. Once comfortable, with the spine straight but not rigid, it is important to breathe using the abdominal muscles. If the mind is not at ease, one should concentrate on a certain point, say on the opposite wall, to focus the mind until it is quiet or "still." Ideally, though, the eyes should remain shut and a state of deep relaxation, or self-hypnosis, should be entered. If this proves impossible, the trainee can breathe—consciously at first—in through the nose and out through the mouth, to release tension in the jaw. Natural breathing will follow.

Uechi Kanyei of Ue-
chi-ryu sitting in a
meditative position.

Post-workout kneel-
ing meditation with
Shorin-ryu teacher
Miyahira Katsuya.

If a state of meditation (*munenmuso*) is, even then, not attainable, it is because the trainee needs to let go of a deep-seated emotional problem that is working its way to the surface and that may not necessarily be known consciously. It is at this stage that a good teacher can spot the potential release and use the proper therapeutic technique, such as shiatsu massage, to act as a catalyst and assist in inducing and regulating an emotional release. Some of these mental blocks are due to past-life phenomena and, being deep in the subconscious, may seem to be difficult to let go of. Even then, if the precept of "Relax, Release, and Let Go" is adhered to, the soul will eventually find a way—it holds the key to healing itself. When a trainee follows these simple steps and practices with diligence over a number of years, the body and the mind will be in a fit state for enlightenment, which will come about naturally, sometimes quite suddenly.

The intellectual key is therefore to study hard and keep on practicing. Letting go of the clutter of the ego, comes easily, giving the higher self room to enter. A harmonious relationship with one's own true self (not one's navel!) will arise. So, train to open up and be flexible in body, mind, and spirit, accepting others for what they are. Avoid being hard-headed and closed-minded. In a nutshell, albeit a universal one, know yourself and become like a child, "for none but such as these will enter the Kingdom of Heaven"; Heaven being the state of Nirvana, true enlightenment.

A necessary word of warning is to avoid meditating in front of a shrine containing an effigy or other representation of a particular deity, cult figure, or object of reverence. It is also important to remember not to be lured into the worship or senseless veneration of any spiritual being. Spiritual experiences of the subconscious can sometimes be fascinating and quite eye-opening, but must never become the be-all and end-all of one's labors. They, like dreams, should be looked upon objectively, without forgetting the sometimes harsh reality of the physical world, and should never become an excuse for denying that reality. Chanting can often be rewarding, but is not a path to enlightenment in itself, and one should know exactly what the words of the chant mean. To summarize, Zen is about self-discovery, enlightenment, and freedom, not about dark, binding religious doctrines and oppressive dictates, which can be stagnating to the soul.

2

Stone Age Weapons
and History

The Ryukyu Islands stretch like a gargantuan knotted rope tossed into a sea in a long sway for well over one thousand kilometers, connecting the island of Kyushu (Japan) in the north, to Taiwan in the south. There are approximately 105 islands in the chain. More than twenty-five of these are mere uninhabited waterless islets, or infertile rocky outcrops on the expansive coral reefs—the proverbial desert islands. However, many of the larger islands are extremely fertile. They are usually thickly forested, except on the low-lying areas and coastal plains where the forest cover has been cleared for habitation and to make way for the growing of sugar cane, rice, and other cash crops. Geologically, the islands were formed during the Tertiary Period when a series of depressions appeared in what is now the East China Sea. They arc in a convex curve along the line of the continental shelf, within the offshore buttresses of the protective barrier reefs, as if, in the past, the boundary of the civilized world had put up an outward eastern defense against the sometimes violent Pacific Ocean. The much-eroded and

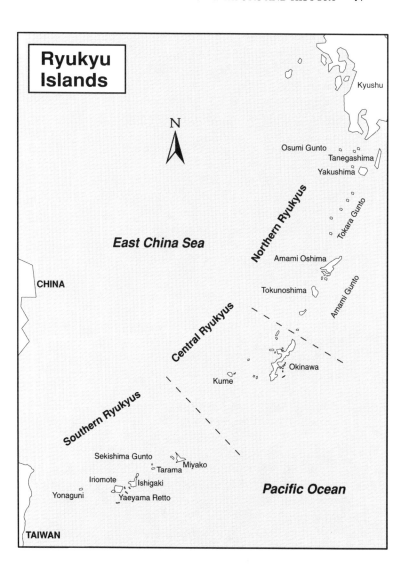

Ryukyu Islands

N

Kyushu

Osumi Gunto
Tanegashima
Yakushima

Northern Ryukyus

Tokara Gunto

East China Sea

Amami Oshima

CHINA

Tokunoshima

Amami Gunto

Central Ryukyus

Okinawa

Kume

Southern Ryukyus

Sekishima Gunto
Tarama
Miyako
Iriomote
Ishigaki
Yonaguni
Yaeyama Retto

Pacific Ocean

TAIWAN

broken landscapes are interspersed by a variety of rock formations, from towering granite mountain massifs, to red sandstone slopes and jagged limestone escarpments.

Historically, the division of the chain into three geographical groups, the Northern, Central, and Southern Ryukyus, has been relevant to the cultural development of the islands as a whole, as well as to that of the Stone Age tools and weapons. The Northern Ryukyus consist of the Amami Gunto, Tokara Gunto, and Osumi Shoto; the main island of these three groups being Amami Oshima. The Central Ryukyus are Okinawa Island and its satellite islands (Okinawa Gunto), like Kume Island and Kudaka Island; while the Southern Ryukyus are made up of the Miyako and Yaeyama Island groups (Sakishima Gunto). With a total land area of 1,256 square kilometers, Okinawa Island is by far the largest in the Ryukyuan chain, almost twice as big as the runner-up, Amami Oshima. By an accident of nature, or a fault in geological design, the Ryukyus were, in the days when prehistoric folk settled them, divided into two distinct and separate cultural units. The more advanced, older culture of the Northern and Central Ryukyus was unknown to the primitive islanders in the Southern Ryukyus until around 1000 A.D., because the peoples were separated by an awesome barrier—the open sea.

Navigable waterways have always been an enhancement to trade and the spread of new ideas, whereas unnavigable waterways have prevented such intercourse. Modern salesmen and tourists, armed with briefcases and Canon cameras, can safely travel unhindered up and down the Ryukyu Islands in high-tech jets and car ferries with all the latest Japanese technological navigational aids and weather satellite equipment keeping a watchful electronic eye on any approaching storms. However, the Stone Age traders and settlers of prehistory had to rely on sea currents, intuition, and their own eyesight to spot landmarks and note changing weather conditions. Coastal navigation was the safest way to travel by sea, with island-hopping for anyone more adventurous. Open-sea travel was far too dangerous.

Paddling north from the Philippine Islands then, utilizing the north-moving Kuroshio currents, the early seamen in their crude dugout canoes would, over a number of years perhaps, work their way through the Babuyan and Batan Island groups, to Botel Tobago (Lan Yu) and Lu Dao, then across to the coast of Eastern Taiwan. Making their way up the coast of this enormous island in stages, they would arrive at a point near the northern end, where, if they headed towards the rising sun, they could reach the westernmost of the Sakishima Islands, namely Yonaguni. On a clear day, the massive mountains of Taiwan would still be clearly and comfortably behind them.

Heading due east from Yonaguni, after choosing the weather carefully, our early sailors would have reached a point at which the jungle-covered mountains of Iriomote Island, to the west, would come into sight, while the stark gray plateaus and cliffs of Yonaguni gradually faded over the horizon and disappeared into the sunset. On reaching the safe, sandy shores of Iriomote, the canoeists would paddle on through the tranquil, shallow inland sea of the Yaeyama Islands to Ishigaki. Then they would cross the fairly sheltered sea to Tarama Island and finally arrive at the comparatively large island of Miyako. But that was the end of the line. The nearest island further on, to the northeast, was Okinawa, but the distance between the two islands, 282 kilometers, was far too great to cover in primitive craft and the seas were too turbulent. Even if castaways had drifted north on the Kuroshio to the Central or Northern Ryukyus, they would not have been able to make the return journey. Their influence on the more developed culture of the northern islands would have been minimal, if anything.

In similar fashion to the southern sea route up to Miyako, the northern trade or immigration route, down from Korea, through Tsushima to Kyushu and on down the Northern and Central Ryukyus, was fairly navigable for early sailors by island-hopping, but ended on the southern tip of Okinawa Island at the very same 282 kilometer sea barrier. The result was that, in the prehistoric era, the development and technology of the Southern Ryukyu Islands of Sakishima was (until about A.D. 1000) influenced only by the primitive southern cultures, with no recognized influences from the Okinawan or Japanese islands to the north. Rough stone implements of the Neolithic Period found in the Sakishima Islands resemble those found in Southeast Asia. They consist of pecked hammerstones, with an abundance of chipped or semi-polished, oval cross-sectioned adzes similar to those found on Eastern Taiwan. Some fully polished quadrangular adzes have also been unearthed and these are identical to those found on Palawan Island in the Philippines.

No one yet knows exactly when the first people arrived on the Sakishima Islands, but a date of 6000 B.C. has been put forward. Their crude implements were used primarily for hunting deer, wild boar, dugong, and turtles, as well as for fishing. Agricultural tools were probably employed at a later date for primitive farming, but no Chinese or Japanese artifacts predating A.D. 1000 have been found. Whether or not these hunting, manufacturing, and farming implements were used as weapons to settle intertribal, family, or boundary disputes, or for personal protection is known only to the people who employed them and will most likely remain their secrets. That there were rudimentary stylized combatant techniques used by Stone Age peoples living in the Pacific area has been widely documented in the last several hundred years by European seafarers. Ferdinand Magellan met his fate on the Philippine Islands in 1521 and Captain Cook was dispatched by Hawaiian natives in 1779 when he inadvertently introduced them to the Iron Age. Ten years later, following the Mutiny on the Bounty, Captain William Bligh and his men almost met with a similar fate on their odyssey to Timor in H.M.S. Bounty's longboat when they anchored at a Melanesian island for supplies.

Such effective butchering techniques have even survived, as cultural entities, into the modern era among people descended from the Polynesian colonists of New Zealand; as well as among people of Micronesian, Melanesian, and Malay ancestry, who had the same forebearers as those who entered the Southern Ryukyus during its Stone Age. Spectacular displays of their onetime fighting prowess regularly thrill tourists from Auckland to Manila, however, even if there were combatant techniques developed or practiced by Stone Age folk living on any of the Southern Ryukyu Islands before A.D. 1000, these did not survive into the modern era. Neither, if they had existed, could they have affected the development of either Te or Kobudo to anything more than the remotest degree. Te and Kobudo were developed on Okinawa Island, so it is on this island and the various cultures that have influenced it that we must focus our attention.

Archaeological evidence shows that the earliest Homo Sapiens known to have lived anywhere in the Ryukyu Islands did so in the Northern and Central Ryukyus at least 30,000 years ago. It is believed that they moved down across land bridges from the north during a time when the ocean level was much lower than it is now, but could not penetrate further south because of the sea barrier, which was in existence even then. Remains of these people, *Yamashita dokutsu-jin* (Yamashita Cavemen), were unearthed in a cave at Yamashita in what is now the thriving commercial center of downtown Naha City, the capital of Okinawa Prefecture. Human bones, carbon-dated to approximately 16000 B.C. were also excavated from a deep fissure at a limestone quarry near Minatogawa Village in Gushichan Ward, on the southern end of Okinawa Island; the poor soul to whom they belonged had either fallen down this pit, been pushed into it, or had his body dumped there. Both the peoples that these two individuals represent lived by hunting, using bone, deer antler, and rough stone implements, which may indicate they led a migratory existence.

The Okinawan Shell Mound Era (2000 B.C.–A.D. 616)

From 2000 B.C., the Central Ryukyu Islands entered a phase of development, still technically in the Stone Age, but appropriately termed the Shell Mound Era. It started to end in about A.D. 616. More than 450 shell mounds of this era have been discovered and investigated on Okinawa and its satellite islands, with three different chronological divisions being recognized:

> Early Shell Mound Era: 2000 to 500 B.C.
> Middle Shell Mound Era: 500 to 100 B.C.
> Late Shell Mound Era: 100 B.C. to A.D. 616

The development of culture on Okinawa during the Early Shell Mound period is thought to have been influenced by an immigrant element from the north that came by sea. Nijo Heikosenmon earthenware was manufactured locally and is thus represented as being indigenous, but, at a later stage, more and more seafaring peoples must have come down from, or through, the Northern Ryukyus. The influence of the more advanced Kyushu culture began to be felt, as is testified by several shards of Ichiki-style earthenware (of Kyushu origin) that were excavated from a shell mound at Urasoe. The populace used well-made, polished stone tools, bows and arrows, harpoons, and refined boar-tusk, shell, and bone implements, such as ornamental hair pins and charms. They lived by hunting wild boars, as well as by fishing and gathering seafood from the beaches and lagoons.

Physical evidence of Chinese-influenced plaques, or pendants, from shell mounds at Attabaru (1400 B.C.), Yaejima (710 B.C.), Kadena, and Sachihija, all on Okinawa Island, demonstrate that continuous contact, indirect at least, by island-to-island trade, was being made with Chinese cultural spheres during this period.

In the shell mounds of the Middle Shell Mound period of Okinawa (500–100 B.C.), shells and animal bones are not so common, seeming to indicate that the people living on Okinawa Island at this time tended to shy away from the seashore for some reason. The staple foods became berries, fruits, and plants. Based on finds of artifacts bearing Taotie monster-mask-like designs, from a burial site on Tane Island (Tanegashima) in the Northern Ryukyus off Kyushu, some suggestions have been made that fugitives from China during the Warring States Period (475–221 B.C.), fled persecution and raided the unprotected Northern or even Southern Ryukyu Islands.

No evidence exists of Chinese settlement, but there is proof that artifacts from some areas of China reached as far south as the Central Ryukyus by stray contact. From a shell mound at Gusukudake, just south of Naha, some third century B.C. knife-shaped North Chinese bronze coins (*meitosen* in Japanese, *mingdaoqian* in Chinese) of great significance were excavated. They indicate that a fragment of the Bronze Age had arrived on Okinawa, albeit via the back door, because the coins were probably traded across to Kyushu from Korea, then on down through the Ryukyu Island chain from settlement to settlement. Such coins were produced in the Kingdom of Yen that collapsed in 265 B.C., but which, according to the *Shanhaijing* (*Classic of Mountains and Waterways*) had trade relations with the Wo (Wa in Japanese), the people of Kyushu. Between 221 and 210 B.C., some time after the revolution that destroyed Yen, the emperor Qin reorganized Chinese society by centralizing the authority and creating an empire. Qin (Chin), from whom China got her name, had wanted to start history anew by burning all records of the past. He had also desired to uncover the secrets of alchemy so that base metals could be changed into gold.

Another of Qin's pet quests was to try to discover the secrets of immortality by sending exploratory expeditions to the distant islands in the East China Sea, which he and his contemporaries believed were inhabited by "happy immortals." Thus, in the year 219 B.C., a mission of several ships carrying a selection of seeds and about three thousand young men, women, and craftsmen set out for the islands toward the east. None of these ships made the return voyage, so their exact landfall was not recorded. Many historians now believe that they ended up in Southern Korea and Western Kyushu, affecting the development of the Wo and bringing them closer to the civilized world. With them would have arrived Daoist ideals and possibly the introduction of advanced weaponry with stylized martial arts (Wushu). As for Qin, he may have had his eccentricities and failures, but one thing that he did do right, perhaps, was to set in motion the groundwork for the development of the powerful Han dynasty (206 B.C.–A.D. 220) that followed shortly after his death.

During the initial phases of Okinawa's Late Shell Mound period (100 B.C.–A.D. 616), while the island was still largely cut off from the rest of the world, the influence of the Chinese was being felt as far away as the Roman Empire, with which the Han was developing good trade relations via Persian middlemen. Chinese military expeditions had reached the borders of India, with Indochina and northern parts of Korea also beginning to feel the benefits of regular trade. By 166 A.D., a delegation from Rome had arrived on the Chinese coast by ship.

In 57 A.D., when the first visit to China by Japanese Wo people was noted, the world was indeed getting smaller and the inhabitants of Okinawa Island were being pulled ever closer toward it. Quite naturally, the Han Chinese confused the Ryukyu Islanders with the Wo, still believing in the old romantic Daoist tales that the Eastern Islanders had eternal life—rather like nineteenth-century European romanticists who, ignoring the reality of the sordid social strife of the Polynesians, preferred to believe that the Hawaiian Islands were the epitome of a blissful paradise. The Han had wanted to discover from where the source of life sprang, but the truth of the matter was that the Okinawan Islanders still lived from hand to mouth, eking out a simplistic Neolithic lifestyle; most of their weapons and tools being very basic Stone Age technology. In this Late Shell Mound period, though, settlements in the Central Ryukyus were established on or near sand dunes, or in large sheltering caves by the seashore, indicating a certain amount of security. The increasing population now engaged widely in fishing for a livelihood and imported Yayoi-type pottery from the Kyushu area, showing that yet another immigrant band had come down from somewhere north. They had probably taken up home and interbred with the locals, as migrant people (including myself) have done for thousands of years.

It is important to note that, from its outset, the Yayoi culture of Japan proper (300 B.C.–A.D. 300) had the use of imported iron weapons, as well as iron implements used in wet-rice farming. Iron swords, arrow heads, and knives of this era have been uncovered there, along with bronze (which came in later) glaives, swords, hand spears, and bells. No such valuable iron or bronze artifacts of this period have ever been found on or near Okinawa Island, so we can safely assume the martial arts, as we know them today, had not yet arrived either. Metal weapons had simply not been imported, let alone used for waging wars or even for ceremonial purposes. Rice had not arrived either, nor had the iron tools necessary to harvest it successfully.

The Wo people of the Yayoi culture in Kyushu had been divided into many independent settlements, some of which were trading with the Chinese at Lelang in Northern Korea. There was much conflict between these various Wo mini-states, or "Queen Counties," but by the second century A.D. a female leader, Himiko, was able to pacify the land and bring about a union between more than thirty settlements. This move lead to better trade and more cultural exchanges among the Chinese and the Wo.

From the latter half of the third century, the Wo were referred to as Yamato and they entered a phase in their development that lasted until the seventh century. This is now labeled the Tumulus or Kofun Age, because of the large number of superb burial mounds found over a large area of modern Japan. Rather than intruding south into the Ryukyus, the now-powerful Yamato, with their superior weaponry, had pushed and pillaged east across the Inland

Sea of Japan, to the fertile plains beyond. From there they had expanded back into the Korean peninsula for a while, but, in the fifth century, the new colonies had been lost and Yamato military power had declined. Eventually a new, peaceful Japanese state (based on Han prototypes and Buddhist concepts) grew up in the Nara area. This was consolidated under the expert leadership of Shotoku Taishi, who lived from 574 to 622 A.D.

Far to the west, the teachings of Jesus of Nazareth had, soon after his murder, been altered, ritualized, and incorporated into a new religion that his followers, as if to appease their own consciences, called Christianity. It contained elements of his brilliant life, but was obsessed with his gory death. In its turn, this organized system of beliefs had been affected by, and now affected, the development of older organized religions that we now call Zoroastrianism and Buddhism, religions which, incidentally, had respectively been based on the teachings of Zoroaster and Siddhartha Gautama (the historical Buddha) and not invented by them. Much of what is listed as, or referred to as Buddhism in Japan and Okinawa Prefecture (or other parts of the world, for that matter) does not necessarily have Siddhartha Gautama or his teachings as its central figure of veneration. A so-called Buddhist sect may, for example, revere the self-born, strangely Christ-like personality of Yakushi Nyorai with his twelve divine helpers, or they may venerate the Japanese-born saint, Nichiren, and not even contemplate Siddhartha. As I mentioned earlier, Mary, the mother of Jesus, appears as Kannon to whom many "Buddhist" temples on Okinawa are dedicated.

What we tend to refer to as Buddhism is therefore a broad term denoting organized religion that contains a mixture of rituals and beliefs from various sources and which reveres any number of saints from various parts of the world, depending on the identity of the particular sect in question. A Buddhist sect may or may not teach or encourage meditative practices or prayer. In the first century A.D., as of today, holding discussions, giving lectures, and proselytizing on various beliefs from different religious or philosophical orders was a popular intellectual pastime among erudite persons. Chinese people were no exception and, as ever, were hungry for the teachings and thirsty for the concepts of such organized religions coming in from the south (India) and west (Rome and Persia). Although they all became lumped together under the term "Buddhism," there was only one real common factor between them—they all contained some principal elements of ancient truths. It was this Buddhism that began working its way into Chinese thought patterns. Centuries-old Daoist and Confucian wisdom was soon affected and, when mixed with the new philosophies, sciences, and ceremonies, they developed into the "isms," Daoism and Confucianism.

In the third century, these revamped organized religions in China were further affected by the onslaught of the teachings of the Persian Mani (or Manes), who claimed descent, through his mother, from the Parthian royal family and who founded Manichaeism. Later, in the mid-fifth century, another wave of organized religion followed suit, again via Persia; this was Nestorian Christianity. It became so popular that when the Persian bishop, Aluoben, reached the Chinese capital Changan in 635 A.D., he was given the task of founding several monasteries—or should we say "Buddhist temples." A number of these Buddhist sects and teachings started to become popular in Japan along with the introduction of Chinese writing and literature that followed the arrival of foreign craftsmen, in the fourth century. The "official" introduction of Buddhism though, via Paekche, Korea, is put at either 538 or 552 A.D. True understanding and enlightenment did not come until the arrival of the two contemporaries Daruma Daishi and Shotoku Taishi.

Until this time, the inhabitants of the Central Ryukyu Islands had been minimally affected by the expanding empires to their north and west. However, a Chinese expedition in search of happy immortals reached Yakushima Island in the Northern Ryukyus in 608. The unhappy islanders refused to give in to the Chinese and a battle ensued, during which a large number of Yakushima Islander captives were taken and transported to China. Along with these prisoners went their confiscated weapons, demonstrating that the Northern Ryukyus were by this time militarized—probably along Japanese lines. The Central Ryukyus, though, were still considered frontier regions.

Kami Jidai, the Realm of Heaven (616–1187)

The people living on Okinawa were recorded by the Yamato for the first time in 616 A.D., when thirty of them from the "Southwestern Islands" were taken to Nara to learn the superior culture at Shotoku Taishi's court, thus marking the beginning of the end of the Shell Mound Era. A few years later, missionaries were sent south to the Central Ryukyus from Nara. They took with them, among other things, rice and the knowledge of how to grow and harvest it. Civilization had arrived on Okinawa's doorstep, along with highly refined arts, music, dancing, education, and meditative martial exercises—probably the precursor of what is now called Te. Iron tools were brought for farming and iron weapons for survival. Unlike most first chapters of history, though, the Iron Age on Okinawa had begun peacefully. Archaeological evidence is scant, but according to tradition, these first colonizing agents originally landed at the tiny, flat island of Kudaka, which lies amidst the barrier reefs off Okinawa's southeastern shore. From there they crossed over to Hyakuna (*lit.,* One Hundred Names) on Okinawa's Chinen Peninsula, near where two perpetual springs, Ukinju-Hainju (*lit.* Silent Water, Running Water), gush life-giving water from the limestone rocks into an area of coastal rice paddies.

Here, to this day, where rice was first planted in Okinawan mud, it is still grown for ritual purposes. According to legends recorded in written form in the sixteenth and seventeenth centuries, the people of Okinawa had lived in caves for thousands of years until these first settlers arrived on the scene. They were "gods and goddesses" who had descended from "Heaven" (Nara, perhaps), planted rice, and built sea barriers by transporting stones and by planting trees. Among them were two key figures, a male, Shinerikyo, and a female, Amamikyo, both of whom are still revered as ancestral deities; they were the progenitors of the Kami Jidai (Realm of Heaven). Amamikyo had actually had a miraculous virgin birth. Before consummating their marriage, she had lived in a house next to Shinerikyo, her husband-to-be, and was impregnated with the help of a divine wind.

The resulting parthenogenetic birth produced a son who became the first ruler of Okinawa island. Their next child, a girl, became the first priestess and their third offspring, another boy, was the first rice farmer. The eldest son appears to have been called Tenteishi, meaning "Son of the Heavenly Emperor." The dynasty he founded lasted for twenty-five generations, finally coming to a violent end in the latter part of the twelfth century. Tenteishi himself sired five children, three boys and two girls. His eldest son was Tenson (appropriately meaning "Heavenly Grandchild"), who followed in his father's footsteps as ruler. The second son became the forerunner of all the Anji (nobles) and the third son took up farming. Tenteishi's daughters became virginal priestesses. Thus Kami Jidai is also called the "The Tenson Era." These first civilized colonizers took up residence in an easily defended area near Hyakuna on the Chinen Peninsula of Okinawa Island, where there are some sheltering caves called Seefa Utaki; arguably the most important ancestral sacred grove on the islands, for most of the present-day populace claim descent from here.

Later, the settlers, or their descendants, moved across the island to the Urasoe/Shuri area where there were good natural harbors and rich, fertile soil. In early spring of 1980, I stood at the northern end of the sandy beach at Hyakuna, where gigantic, jagged lumps of limestone cliff have fallen haphazardly into the sea, providing minimal protection from the elements. With me were Higa Seitoku (founder of the Bugeikan), his son Kiyohiko, daughter Reiko, and some top students. Among them was a friend called Zaan, who was a sensitive, a seer. We were all gazing contemplatively out to sea across the calm of the lagoon facing a stone post that is visible at low tide and marks the exact spot where the settlers landed. There was something in the fresh, warm sea air—the atmosphere was strangely quiet, to say the least. The limpid sea had an oily sheen. Higa Seitoku broke the silence and spoke reverently, murmuring that he was perceiving that "something was happening." A piece of living history was about to come to light. Zaan, with eyes closed, concentrated for a few minutes in a world apart. When he came back to reality, he explained that he had "seen," with his third eye, a clear moving "picture" of a golden dragon-prowed *takara-bune* (treasure ship) heading steadily towards the shore.

From the bow end it reminded him of a Viking longship, but on board were the Shichifukujin, the Seven Gods of

The Shichifukujin (clockwise from the top): Bisha-monten, Fukurokuju, Benzaiten, Ebisu, Daikokuten, Jurojin, and Hotei.

Good Luck. These include: Benzaiten (Skt. Sarasvati), the Goddess of Music and Art; Daikokuten (Skt. Mahakala), the God of Wealth in Japan; and Bishamonten (Skt: Vaisravans), the God of Dignity. Dressed in full armor with a bushy beard and holding a hand spear, Bishamonten is the protector of the righteous and a patron of warriors. The temple town of Shiji, near Oji in the Nara area of Japan, was founded in his honor by Shotoku Taishi, because Bishamon had played a major role in helping him defeat the enemies of Buddhism.

In the quaint Japanese city of Oji, there is a quiet temple, Daruma-ji, said to have been built by order of Shotoku Taishi. It is dedicated to the memory of our old friend Daruma and is one of many such temples in Japan and Okinawa. In the picturesque grounds can be observed two commemorative stones that mark the places where, legend has it, the two most notable intellectual contemporaries of the times, Shotoku Taishi and Daruma Daishi, held Zen *mondo* (question-answer) sessions. Inside the temple building is a central statue of Kannon, flanked on one side by an image of Shotoku Taishi and on the other by a seated wooden statue of Daruma—carved in 1430, though, it is not a true likeness of him. Daruma is also recorded as being associated with Shotoku Taishi in the *Nihon Shoki* (Chronicle of Japan) and the *Genko Shakusho* (Chronicles of Japanese Buddhism), which relate fanciful stories of their meetings. Reliable legend has it that Daruma was born and brought up under the name Bodhidharma at Kanchipuram (Conjeeveram), near Madras in Southern India, during the early sixth century A.D. At this center of world civilization he would have made contact with Middle Eastern traders and been influenced by the teachings of the Buddhist sects of the time and by the Christianity that had been introduced there by St. Thomas five centuries earlier.

Like his sixth-century B.C. predecessor, Siddhartha Gautama, Daruma was born into the *Ksatriya* (warrior) caste and received training in the martial arts from an early age. Also like the historical Buddha, Daruma set out on an enlightening journey into the world of self-discovery that, in his case, initially lasted three years and took him by ship to Canton in Southern China. A little bit later on in life, he turns up at the Shaolin Temple in Henan Province, Northern China, where he introduced a series of martial art-based exercises to the out-of-shape monks who had been putting contemplation before action and words before deeds. He spent nine years in the area, teaching, drinking tea (for which he is also noted), and meditating, facing a blank psychological wall. From the exercises passed on by Daruma, as well as other sources and influences, his devotees and their followers later developed self-defense methods that are known widely today as Shaolin Temple Boxing; the precursor of Kobudo and Karate that entered Okinawa mostly in the nineteenth century.

Daruma supposedly left the Shaolin Temple for reasons known only to himself, and turns up in Japan in his middle age. Here the name Bodhidharma became Bodai Daruma, hence Daruma, or the honorific Daruma Daishi (Eminent Teacher Daruma). Although recognized as a venerated teacher of the martial arts, meditative practices, and therapies, it has not been well established what happened to him in the end, but the Daruma Temple at Oji makes the dubious claim that he is buried there. Noted for his powerfully rounded bulging belly, bright (probably blue) eyes, largish nose, and full beard though, he is, in popular art and culture, still as real as life itself in the heart of every Japanese. His meditative practices (Zen) and healing techniques (now called shiatsu) are practiced by millions daily. On Okinawa, the people who visit the Daruma-ji Temple at Shuri ask him advice, through meditative prayer, on the practical things of life, such as business matters and childbirth. Many students visit the small temple before taking examinations, to help them be more confident, relaxed, and centered on the big day. The white, folded-paper wishes of thousands of hopefuls adorn the branches of the cherry blossom trees outside in the courtyard.

There is no doubt that Shotoku Taishi was influenced by the teachings of Daruma. Born in 574 A.D., Shotoku was a child prodigy who grew up to be an all-round genius and political giant, representing the needs of the everyday people. He was born into high office in a lowly horse shed and was first named Umayado no Miko, which means Prince of the Stable. Another of his names was Toyotomimi no Oji, or Prince Endowed with Intelligence and Judgment. Shotoku Taishi, is his popular posthumous name, meaning Prince of Sagely Virtue, but it came into use in the late eighth century, well after his death. His mother was Anahobe no Hashihito no Himemiko, or Anamiko for short. She was connected to the powerful Soga family, which was prominent in foreign affairs and trade. At the early age of twenty, Shotoku Taishi became the powerful prince regent to the Empress Suiko, virtually taking on the role of prime minister and subsequently organizing society along ethical rather than blood lines. One of his first moves in office, in 594, was to issue an imperial edict calling for the promotion of Buddhism; a "Buddhism" that had been strongly influenced by Daruma's Zen and the aforementioned world-wide known discourses, including Christian teachings.

With the use of imported foreign craftsmen, Shotoku next embarked on a building program of what have now become Buddhist temples, but which were originally intended to be temples of learning; i.e., universities. His role in popularizing his brand of Buddhism was furthered by his writing and publication of texts, such as the *Lotus Sutra*, that helped clarify his ideals and concepts and which conversely affected the development of organized religions back on the continent. In 604, Shotoku Taishi put into action a twelve-colored cap ranking system for the civil service, under which government office could be attained by individual merit; no longer by mere right of birth. The same year saw the introduction of his Seventeen Article Constitution that extolled the chivalrous virtues of harmony, justice, diligence, and decorum. Article 17 of this, in particular, states that all civil servants must refrain from despotic or autocratic means of carrying out affairs of state. The year 600 A.D. had seen a renewal of foreign affairs and trade, with envoys and students being sent to China. More envoys went in 607, when the leader among them delivered a letter from Shotoku cheekily addressed to, "The Emperor of the Land of the Setting Sun," from, "The Ruler of the Land of the Rising Sun."

Among the ordinary people in Japan, Shotoku was noted for having promoted new agricultural and industrial technological innovations, as well as for creating a new infrastructure of roads, bridges, and communications. Particularly, though, he is remembered for implementing a welfare system, with hospitals and homes for the sick, the feeble, and for orphaned children; he even made ordinances for the protection of animal rights. At his hospital and training center complex inside his retreat at Ikaruga (now Horyu-ji Temple), near Nara, he had carved, by the noted sculptor Tori, a statue dedicated to Yakushi Nyorai (Skt: Bhaisajya-guru), the enlightened one who has promised to heal all those sick and weary who have asked for help in his name. This statue, or rather the healing concepts it represents, became the focus of attention at Ikaruga. Today, effigies of

Yakushi Nyorai are especially venerated by the followers of the Shingon, Tendai, and Zen Buddhist sects in Japan and Okinawa, the concepts though have faded with the passing of time. On the personal side of things, Shotoku Taishi brought into government three human elements of the ruler, ministers, and the populace, all mutually respecting one another's positions. In his dealings with everyone, he practiced peace, salvation, and gentle persuasion; dialogue rather than brute force or armed conflict.

A case in point is that he refused to make charges against the confessed murderer of the former emperor, preferring to persuade the guilty party to seek forgiveness of his own wrong deeds, through positive behavioral patterns. In his historical chronologies and records of the Yamato people, Shotoku used the term *Tenno* (Heavenly Sovereign) as opposed to the traditional *Daio* (Great King) and was seen as being the Son of Heaven. Shotoku Taishi officially died in 622, one year after his mother's reported death and, oddly enough, only a month after his favorite consort passed away. As a memorial to him, Tori cast a bronze statue of the Buddha, Shaka (Skt: Shakamuni), in Shotoku's likeness and later the Guze (Savior) Kannon was carved out of wood in the same style. These are still in a remarkable state of preservation and they depict a tall man of slender build, with a large halo about his head; his elongated face has pronounced yet gentle, caring features.

Beautiful sculptures no doubt, but a feeble substitute for the real thing. Life, Zen, and Shotoku were out of fashion, organized Buddhism with its dead imagery, hierarchical priests and fixed dictates was on its way in. But was it? A popular cult that was to last hundreds of years soon developed around the belief that Shotoku Taishi had been a reincarnation of the Savior of Mankind; a continuing process that, it was thought, had followed through from

Zoroaster (or Shaka) and Jesus of Nazareth, both of whom were, confusingly so, revered as different buddhas, or *kannons* under various names. Likewise, Daruma was thought to be an incarnation of the historical Buddha, Siddhartha Gautama; thus grew the confusion of Zen with the Buddhism that had been founded in his name, using his teachings. Another belief was that, due to the mounting dangers to his life from his political opponents, Shotoku, with his wife and mother, had faked their deaths and fled, along with friends and other family members, on a ship to the Southern Islands where they were received as gods. And thus the Amamikyo legend grew. Or was it mere legend? The name of the Goddess Amamikyo is remarkably similar to Shotoku's mother's shortened name, Anamiko, and both their sons were "Sons of Heaven."

Also on board the mythical treasure ship, the Japanese Bounty of antiquity, among the Seven Gods of Good Luck are two gods who are unique to Japan; Jurojin, the God of Longevity, who is depicted as an old man; and Fukuroku-ju, the God of Wisdom, who is depicted as a wise sage— Daruma Daishi and Shotoku Taishi perhaps? Perhaps mere romance, but then again, perhaps not. Whatever the facts of the matter may be, the Zen, and other, teachings introduced to Japan by Daruma Daishi, that were further formulated and put into practice on a government level downwards by Shotoku Taishi as his living interpretation of Buddhism, in the late sixth and early seventh centuries A.D., would have been transplanted to Okinawa, whether directly or indirectly, with the first civilized colonizers. Once sown, the seeds of Daruma's and Shotoku's precepts about forgiveness and salvation and their Christian-like Zen philosophies sprouted and thrived in the settlements at Urasoe and Shuri. From here they spread throughout the Ryukyu Islands, setting the standards, but not necessarily the actions, of decorum for most of the history of the islands, thence forward. One can observe these attitudes to be still clearly prevalent, not only in affairs of prefectural government and education, but in every type of Okinawan human relationship.

Zen thought patterns pervade the atmosphere of every martial arts dojo and sports gym in Okinawa Prefecture— be the instruction in Te, Kobudo, Karate, Chinese Boxing, or even regular wrestling and boxing. It can be stated with certainty that all areas of traditional Shuri culture and its offshoots that have survived into the present, have their main well-sources in the springs of the sparkling Japanese Asuka/Nara period that was founded at the time of Daruma Daishi and Shotoku Taishi. "Okinawa is a time capsule," it has been often remarked, "a living reference book of the Yamato Asuka/Nara period, with a mere sprinkling of other cultures." Shuri Hogen, traditionally the standard dialect of the prefecture's erudite, for example, is directly related to an early offspring of the Japanese language before the latter was heavily affected by Chinese words and phraseology. Most linguists trace the origin of this polite dialect of propriety back at least 1,400 years, to the Yamato upper classes. Classical music derives from the same era. That goes for drama, too. The slow, graceful movements seen in the Seven Shuri Classical Dances are based on and correspond exactly to meditative forms of Te, resembling those practiced at Shotoku's court. Most of all, the maxims such as *"bugei* (martial arts) and Zen are one," or "in martial arts there are no enemies," at the heart of Kobudo and especially Te practice are an exciting reflection of those truly chivalrous yet short-lived times.

During the years that followed Shotoku Taishi's reported death, the Soga clan in Japan gradually sought to take over control of the country. In the cruel coup d'état of 643, they killed off his remaining immediate relatives, including one of his sons, Yamashiro, along with his family. Following Shotoku's teachings to the letter, some had chosen to take the path of non-resistance, rather than to fight and prolong the bloodshed; they are believed to have sacrificed their own few lives to save the lives of many others. Despite the devastating setback to Shotoku Taishi's innovative, fledgling institutions by the Sogas though, a little of what he had accomplished at Nara was rekindled when some of his students returned (purportedly from China) and influenced another coup d'état. That was in 645 and this time it was the almighty Soga's turn to be destroyed. All opposition to the imperial family was wiped out, allowing the "Taika Reforms" to take place. Although it was not exactly what Shotoku Taishi had envisioned, under these reforms a system of centralized government, with an absolute monarch at the top, was inaugurated. Just as with his teachings becoming empty Buddhist ornamentation, a hollow false image of Shotoku Taishi's model state had been created.

After this incident, more and more contacts were made between Nara and the Ryukyu Islands, further affecting the development of Te, martial arts, and the culture there in general. The *Nihon Shoki* records that in 698 a learned courtier, Fumi no Imiko, was sent off on an expedition to the islands, with a military back-up, to claim them as Japanese territory. He probably made it as far as the Northern Ryukyus because, sixteen months later, men from Amami Oshima, Tanegashima, Yakushima, and Tokunoshima paid homage at the Japanese court, presented produce and were rewarded in turn. In 714, the *Nihon Shoki* records Kume Island off Okinawa, as well as Shingaki (possibly Ishigaki) in the Southern Ryukyus. Six years later, in 720, about 230 Ryukyu Islanders took tribute on a trading venture to Nara and were assigned honorary ranks. In 753, Okinawa itself was recorded for the first time in the *Nihon Shoki,* as the site of a shipwreck by an official mission going from Nara to China. By then, the shipping routes that had taken trading missions and envoys back and forth between Japan and China were changing from the northern route, via Tsushima and Korea, to the southern route that followed the course of the Ryukyus down their western edge to Okinawa, then straight across the East China Sea, to the Yangtze River estuary and the Fujian coast.

Ships were wont to call in at the natural havens of Urasoe and Naha harbors on Okinawa Island for victuals, trade, or for shelter from bad weather. Among these include a shipload of Japanese envoys who stopped over on Okinawa for a month on their way back from China, again, it appears in 753 or 754 A.D. An account was written of this stay by one of the high priest Ganjin's students in the book *Daiwajo Toseiden,* which records that the Ryukyus were recognized as being in three distinct groups—the main group, the off-lying islands, and the furthest away, including Hatenoshima, or Hateruma. No one has recorded what effects this cultural exchange had on the populace of Okinawa, but Ganjin (Ch: Jianzhen), who was born in China and educated at Changan and Luoyang, eventually arrived in Japan a blind man and founded the Toshodai-ji Temple in Nara. By transmitting Tang civilization and his Ritsu sect of Buddhism there, he brought a breath of fresh air to what he considered to be the decadent state of Buddhism.

About one hundred years later, a priestly scholar named Chisho (also known as Enchin) made the claim that he had come across man-eating cannibals when he was stranded for a while somewhere in the Ryukyu Islands (probably the yet-undeveloped Southern Ryukyus) on his way back to Japan from China. At other times, uncontrollable or unwanted ambitious leaders, thought to be trouble makers, were banished from the main Japanese islands and would take refuge or make their residences on Okinawa, introducing the latest ideas into the community. The development of the comparatively peaceful Tenson dynasty of Okinawa was constantly affected in this way and came to its bitter end when the last king of the line was assassinated in 1187 by a disloyal retainer named Riyu. He in turn was quickly dispatched by his successor Shunten, the son of an Okinawan lord's daughter and Tametomo, the noted Japanese warrior. To compound this, in 1186, Shimazu Tadahiza was appointed as the lord of the Japanese fief of Southern Kyushu (Satsuma) by the central Japanese authorities and was granted title over the Twelve Southern Islands in 1206, which included Okinawa. An era of petty feudal barons and constant infighting between them had begun.

A Time of Feudal Castles (1187–1429)

Archaeologically speaking, from about 950 onwards, Okinawa Island entered a new stage of development. For reasons of security, an upper stratum of society started to move more and more away from the exposed seashore settlements into small fortified, hilltop manor houses called *gusuku* (or *gushiku*), for which this era, "Gusuku Jidai" is named. Such dwellings gave the inhabitants limited protection from typhoons and the raids of sea scavengers; they also provided a separate area in which to store trade goods and entertain merchants from overseas. Even now *gusuku* appears in many Okinawan place names and common surnames, Japanized of late to *jo, shiro, ki,* or *gi;* as in Kinjo (Kanagusuku, or "Gold castle"), Tomishiro (Tomigusuku, or "Rich castle"), Tamaki (Tamagusuku, or "Jewel castle"), and Miyagi (Miyagusuku, or "Palace castle"). Rice and wheat became cultivated island-wide during the Gusuku

Era and Sueki Earthenware was imported from Japan proper. Gradually, villages concentrated around the slopes near the bottom of the *gusuku,* which began to develop into larger elaborate forts. Eventually grand stone castles, complete with impressive fortifications were built further inland on top of strategically located hills.

By the eleventh and twelfth centuries the population was increasing rapidly, a new type of pottery, *Fensa Joso-shiki* earthenware, was being produced, and cattle were being raised. More importantly, iron tools and weapons were being manufactured and extensively used. On the Japanese mainland, much had been happening since the Taika Reforms of 645 A.D., as things grew from bad to worse in the political arena. Hereditary emperors had become extremely cloistered and consequently a powerful warrior class had developed in the provinces. They gradually established themselves in or around the new capital city of Kyoto, acting as military policemen. This nouveau samurai class associated with the aristocracy and eventually two rival family lines emerged from it. One group was the Minamoto, or Genji family, who claimed descent from the Emperor Seiwa. The other were the Taira, or Heike, claiming descent from the Emperor Kammu.

Tametomo and his family, who supported the Genji, had been bitter enemies of the Taira. Stories of the times describe him as a boisterous, troublesome youth, noted for his strength and large stature. Because of these assumed difficult and uncontrollable attributes, his father had him transferred to a distant outpost in Kyushu, where he associated with the governor and was given the title of General & Superintendent. Soon after marrying the governor's daughter in 1156, he joined up with some Minamoto followers for an attack on the Taira, but, unfortunately for them, they were on the losing side. After being captured,

The gate at Shuri Castle leading to the burial place of Tametomo.

Tametomo was tortured and banished to the Japanese islands off the Izu Peninsula.

Legend takes over from here and tells us that in about 1165 he somehow escaped from these islands by ship and headed south, ending up in Okinawa, where the Lord of Ozato Castle took him under his wing and married him off to one of his daughters. Shunten, the future king of Okinawa and founder of a new dynasty, was born of this union in 1166, but before Tametomo could enjoy the fruits of his love-making, he was to lead his men on a suicidal attack against the Vice-Governor of Izu on the island of Oshima in Sagami Bay, back up north in Japan proper. Meanwhile, his Okinawan wife and son took up residence in Urasoe overlooking the harbor where they had said their last farewells. Here they waited for the return of Tametomo, giving the name Machi-minato (Waiting Harbor) to the narrow, rock-strewn inlet. A white concrete church surrounded by a plush green lawn and skirted by the busy Highway No. 1 now stands on the rocky outcrop where they waited for so long in vain.

It was Tametomo's nephew, Minamoto Yoritomo, who finally destroyed the Taira family's grip on Japanese politics in 1186. The Minamoto family had been quietly building up their strength in the provinces, while the Taira family had felt secure in the capital. Yoritomo, who had grown up in exile at Izu, was able to rally support for the Minamoto cause and sent his two younger brothers to lead a successful attack against the Taira at Kyoto. The defeated Taira forces were to flee in retreat towards the Inland Sea of Japan, where they regrouped for a while but were finally routed in a land and sea battle off the island of Shikoku—a series of battles that is equal in fame in every Japanese schoolchild's mind as the Battle of Hastings or the Battle of Bunker Hill is to his or her British or American counterparts.

Although some Taira adherents went into hiding among the remote mountain areas of Japan, many headed south by ship to Kyushu and the Ryukyu Islands beyond. Some of these made landfall at Amami Oshima in the Northern Ryukyus, where there stands to this day a monument to Taira Kiyomori's second son. Other fleeing Taira adherents cautiously skirted the Central Ryukyus and made final landfall in the less-developed Southern Ryukyu Islands, introducing their advanced culture, weaponry, and military tactics to the inhabitants, who were still half in the Stone Age. Here, on Miyako, Tarama, Ishigaki, and Yonaguni Islands in particular, traces of their history and traditions remain in the people's faces, customs, festivals, and in stories told about them. Horses descended from those brought by the Taira roam on Yonaguni Island, where *Yamato-haka,* Japanese graves of yore linked to Taira refugees, can also be seen. Some contemporary historians consider the Central Ryukyu Islanders to be of the Minamoto bloodline and the Southern Ryukyu Islanders of Taira stock—a simplistic, convenient classification whereby the Shimazu of Satsuma were able to demand more tribute from the descendants of the Taira refugees.

Like his notorious father Tametomo, Shunten was an energetic youth, but easily won respect as a promising leader among the populace of Okinawa Island. At the age of fifteen, he was chosen by general agreement to take over as Lord of Urasoe Castle and, at about twenty-two years of age, he led the popular revolt against his father's assassin Riyu, allowing him to assert his authoritative guidance over the whole island for fifty-one years. In about 1238, Shunten was succeeded by his son, Shunba Junki, who ruled for eleven years, making his castle at Shuri by updating the older *gusuku* that had been established there centuries earlier. He also introduced the latest phonetic Japanese *hiragana* script, replacing to an extent the older Chinese-character writing system brought by the educated settlers from Japan in the seventh century.

In the fifth year of his reign, a Chinese junk drifted onto an Okinawan coral reef and was greeted somewhat cautiously, as can be ascertained from a depiction of the event in the form of a factual cartoon by a Chinese priest who had been on board the junk. Close observation of this drawing reveals that Okinawans of the time used *sabani* (sampans) as war canoes, each with a square shield at the bow protecting an archer and paddled by a number of men using *eku*-type paddles like those seen in modern Kobudo and Te practice. Standing behind the archers are figures holding metal weapons in their right hands. This is a clear indication that at this time, approximately 1243 A.D., martial arts with well-made, bladed weapons had developed into organized military arts, but it is also important to note, although presumably due to their haste of departure from the shore and lack of any fear about the crew of the junk, the seeming absence of any body armor. The occupants of the war canoes are depicted being dressed in everyday *bashofu* robes—a course, brown material, suited to the climate, that is made from the stem of a species of banana.

In 1249, Shunba Junki was succeeded by his eldest son Gihon, who, taking the blame for several natural calamities, later abdicated to allow the young lord Eiso to attain office. Eiso was a strong leader who rebuilt Urasoe Castle and expanded Okinawan sovereignty so that by 1264 he was accepting tribute from the off-lying islands of Kerama, Kume, and Iheya, as well as from Amami Oshima in the Northern Ryukyus. On Okinawa itself, he introduced a regular taxation system in grain, cloth, and (notably) weapons; he also reorganized land distribution and is thought to have built and maintained storehouses for grain and weaponry. To help with the paperwork involved in the administration of his new outer fiefs, an administrative office was built in 1267, near the port of Tomari in Naha Harbor, at the bottom of the hill that leads up to Shuri Castle—the village of Tomari that grew up around the administrative office is still an important commercial center incorporated, as is Shuri, into greater Naha City.

By 1292, the year Marco Polo left China on his return voyage, it would appear that tiny Okinawa's comparatively high standard of living and military expertise had become noteworthy in the world, because, in that year, Kublai Khan sent a message to King Eiso ordering Okinawa to submit to the Mongols and contribute weapons and manpower towards his proposed invasion of Japan through the Korean Peninsula. Eiso refused, but four years later demands were again made by envoys from the Mongol Court; Eiso again refused to comply, the use of arms was resorted to and a battle ensued. When the aggressors were eventually driven off, they took with them about 130 Okinawan prisoners—their fate has never been discovered.

Eiso reigned until 1300, being succeeded by his son Taisei, grandson Eiji in 1309, and great-grandson Tamagusuku in 1314. The latter was nineteen years of age when he was thrust into office and his inability as a leader soon lost any loyalty he may have inherited. The result was rebellion and Okinawa Island became divided into three feudal states known as the Three Kingdoms—Chuzan, Nanzan, and Hokuzan. Powerful and prosperous Chuzan, the Middle Kingdom in the central region, was controlled from the well-fortified Urasoe and Shuri Castles. Nanzan, the Southern Kingdom in the south, was taken over by the Lord of Ozato who built his new castle on a rounded hillock near what is now the busy fishing port of Itoman. The comparatively large but poor Northern Kingdom, Hokuzan, in the north, was controlled from the massive, granite walls of Nakijin Castle, commanding a prominent position on the mountainous Motobu Peninsula overlooking the natural safe haven of picturesque Unten Harbor.

The lesser Anji lived in smaller strongholds on the wooded hilltops (which even today protrude above the lands and villages the former occupiers once controlled) by extorting heavy taxes with the force of arms. Ancient ceremonies connected with martial arts are sometimes held at these historic sites and the mossy stones of sacred groves, important to the religious function of village and island life, can be easily traced amid the tangle of the jungle creepers. The earthworks, or rubble-strewn ruins, of over one hundred

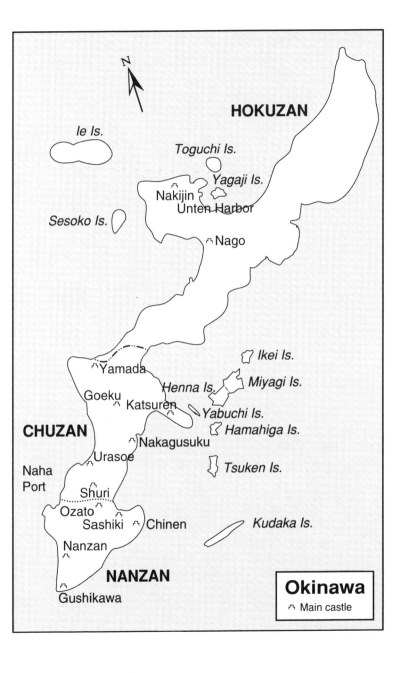

castles and *gusuku* can still be found, mostly concentrated in southern *(nanbu)* and central *(chubu)* Okinawa Island, although there are a few in the north *(hokubu)* and on the outer islands. On studying the design and construction of the larger fortifications built at this time, it is easy to ascertain that they generally had walls and ramparts built in a series of irregular, sometimes concentric, rings, squares, or rectangles, that often hugged the natural contours of the hills and crags in layers, like enormous farming terraces.

Although some castles and *gusuku* had wooden ramparts, the jumbled remains of many once-proud, but now crest-fallen and forlorn stone walls, can be clearly distinguished at the more important sites. Roughly cut, or completely unhewn locally quarried stone was preferred for construction of most of the castles. Due to its availability, limestone was the most commonly used stone in the south and central area of Okinawa, with hard, uncut granite slabs in the north and outer islands—including the Southern Ryukyus. The homely, thatched, wooden houses with thick, hardwood pillars resting on hefty, asymmetrical blocks of sandstone, were the main living quarters of the head family and were usually constructed in the most central enclosure, with the cruder outer buildings for weapon storage, retainers and horses at consecutively lower levels. To prevent damage from the regular annual invasion of typhoons, all wooden buildings were snuggled neatly in the lee of the sturdy castle walls.

The Three Kingdoms was an era when weapons, their users, and their military tactics were put to the ultimate life-and-death test. Te-based martial arts were refined and polished for killing. Honed to a fine cutting edge, they meant survival on a practical level. Many castles and *gusuku*, for example, had a sheer cliff on one or more sides, forcing would-be attackers to advance along previously prepared, but easily defensible positions. Heavily armed longbowmen would be in hiding behind the single, long parapet, ready to spring a surprise retaliatory blow on those attackers who had been lured into the trap. Once inside the castle, any invaders could be mowed down by experts wielding swords, glaives, or hand spears. Horses were used extensively for building castles, for travel to and from other castles, and in military tactics, as can be deduced from examining the remaining sloping steps inside castle walls, that were easily accessible for both mounted and unmounted warriors alike. Water, however, was the essential survival factor during a long siege and all castles, as well as *gusuku,* worth their salt would have a ready, natural supply within the castle walls. Some castles have precipitous steps leading down over thirty meters to large cavernous wells or perpetual springs. Other castles even boasted secret escape routes through natural or man-made caverns.

Tamagusuku kept control of Chuzan, by far the most powerful of the Three Kingdoms, until his death in 1349. He was followed by Sei-i, who in turn was succeeded, in 1350, by Satto, the former governor of Urasoe district. Satto's reign of nearly half a century is important because during his term, Chuzan, while keeping its contacts with Japan, became a tributary state of China, setting the precedent for a triangular relationship that was to last for more than five hundred years. For example, a Buddhist temple, the Gokoku-ji, was founded by a Japanese priest in 1367 at Naminoue headland, overlooking the trading vessels coming and going from Naha harbor to China.

Once formally recognized as King of Chuzan by the Ming court, though, Satto was able to widen the doors for much-needed foreign trade, the lifeblood of tiny Chuzan. Official missions came and went with the Chinese regularly demanding fifty or sixty of the small type of horse found on

Tokara and Yonaguni Islands, as well as sulfur for making gunpowder from Iwojima, far to the east of Okinawa. In 1372 the tribute was rewarded with fine silks, but the Okinawan traders asked for ceramics and iron instead. Thus the next envoy, in 1374, received 70,000 pieces of ceramics and 1,000 pieces of iron. Chuzan, no doubt, was preparing an arms build up on a massive scale.

Eventually a permanent Okinawan settlement was established amongst the international community of Arab Moslems, Malays, Indians, and Siamese at the trading port of Fuzhou on the Fujian coast of China. This meant that a few of the latest foreign customs and manners were imitated in the Chuzan court, later bringing some superficial social and cultural changes in the life of the Okinawan commoners.

Following in Chuzan's footsteps, both Nanzan and Hokuzan sought and attained the right to be recognized as tributary states of mighty China. In 1390, the Southern Ryukyu Islands of the Miyako and Yaeyama groups became tributary states of Chuzan, but had already made direct contacts with China. From 1372 onwards, scholarly youths of upper-class *shizoku* backgrounds were often selected to enroll in the Chinese schools for foreign students at Nanjing or Beijing, where they were drilled in classical arts, culture, history, and ethics, returning to high positions in government in Chuzan—however, there is no record of such scholars learning martial arts in China, and it is doubtful if they did. Under direct decree of the Ming court, in 1393, the "Thirty-Six Families" of Chinese immigrants, including clerks and craftsmen, settled at Kume-mura near Naha. They brought with them, among other trades, badly needed new techniques of shipbuilding and administration, but they were ordinary folk and not of the warrior class, and probably introduced no new martial art systems to

Okinawa. However, from that time onward, Okinawans were able to build their own ocean-going vessels and Chuzan became a center of trade for the whole area.

After Satto's death in 1396, his eldest son, Bunei, carried on the trade relationship as middleman between Japan and China, expanding trade with Southeast Asian countries and Korea. He also had constructed new reception halls, a trading center, and warehouses at Naha, where people from many nations now met and mingled. In 1406, Hashi, a former Anji of Sashiki Castle, taking advantage of the state of confusion at the Chuzan court, deposed Bunei in a military coup d'état and became the self-styled ruler of Chuzan, proclaiming his father to be king. Hashi took over the old castle at Shuri and by 1416 he had taken Nakijin Castle, submitting the ordinary people of Hokuzan in the north to his rule, while many of Bunei's faithful retainers committed ritual suicide. Then, in 1429, he reunified Okinawa, after over one hundred years of bloody internal turmoil and conflict, with a swift and decisive successful strike against Nanzan Castle in the south. Although some violent times still lay ahead, a comparatively peaceful new golden age of international trade, diplomacy, and religious revival was about to begin.

The Golden Age of Trade

Founder of the First Sho Dynasty, Sho Hashi, as Hashi was wont to be titled, was committed to increasing trade with Korea and Southeast Asia (Patani, Java, Sumatra, and Siam) and consequently enlarged the Okinawan settlement at Fuzhou, building a trading depot with reception rooms, warehouses, and residential buildings staffed by Okinawans. Bladed weapons came to occupy a peacekeeping rather than peacemaking status and an ever-increasing profitable role in Okinawan society, as highly prized Japanese swords and other weapons were exported and resold at high prices on the lucrative Chinese and Southeast Asian markets. Okinawa was soon to become a booming crossroads of the East, rivaling the city states of Venice and Genoa in the West or Goa in India. The castle at Shuri was made into the seat of government under Sho Hashi and enlarged into a magnificent building with ornamental ponds and a beautifully constructed, red-lacquered palace at its highest point, overlooking the growing metropolis of Naha. The castle remained almost unchanged until 1945.

The death of Sho Hashi in 1439 saw his second son, Sho Chu, take his father's place. However, he ruled for only five years and was succeeded by his son, Sho Shitatsu, who also lasted five years. Then Sho Hashi's fifth son, Kimpuku (the road builder), came and went in only three years, and was succeeded, after a blood-stained succession dispute, by Sho Hashi's seventh son, Sho Taikyu. The latter was noted especially for his Japanese-style Buddhism and it was during his reign that the economically powerful Zen Buddhist foundation of Tenryu-ji built its branch temple at Shuri, along with the Manju-ji at Sueyoshi near Shuri, which, like the Gokoku-ji temple at Naminoue, was of the Shingon sect. Two other temple orders, the Kogen-ji and the Fumon-ji, were also established during Sho Taikyu's reign.

Although greatly lessened in scope and scale, open rebellion was still a nagging threat. In one tale of loyalty it is written that the Anji of Katsuren Castle, the evil Amawari, was discovered by Gosamaru, the saintly lord of Nakagusuku Castle, to be planning a coup against Sho Taikyu in Shuri. Gosamaru dutifully, but quietly, began to muster his men together to prevent Amawari's warriors from marching down on Shuri, but in the meantime, Amawari, in a brilliant piece of counterespionage, got false intelligence through to the king that it was Gosamaru who was planning the attack on Shuri Castle. As a result, all the king's horses and all the king's men trundled off and trustingly launched an all-out attack on Gosamaru at Nakagusuku. Rather than take up arms against their respected king though, Gosamaru and his men disemboweled themselves inside the castle walls.

Disappointingly, Nakagusuku Castle was burnt down, never to be rebuilt, but, as a memorial to Gosamaru, his magnificent tomb lies below the adjacent hull-shaped crag of Daigusuku that looks as if it is going to set sail across Nakagusuku Bay. At Nakagusuku Castle there is a plaque written in English (in itself a bit of American occupation-era history) that records the following:

Nakagusuku Castle was built during the turbulent period in Okinawa's history when clan warfare was common and the Three Kingdoms were unified by the king at Shuri. Lord Gosamaru, skilled in battle as well as construction, erected this largest and last of the fortresses about 1448 on the foundation of an earlier fortification. The castle buildings were destroyed on August 15, 1458 as a result of the mysterious court intrigue that resulted in the death of Lord Gosamaru. Only the ramparts and dwelling foundations remain today. The design offers an excellent example of sturdiness and strength and the castle is well known for the lineal beauty of its stone placement work. Its construction preceded by eighty years the first stone Japanese castles—an accomplishment of which Okinawans can be justly proud.

And the fate of the wicked Amawari? Well, when his

dastardly plot was discovered, he was promptly slaughtered by the king's men within his own stronghold at Katsuren.

King Sho Taikyu's extravagance, lavished on temple-building, metal-casting, and elaborate entertainment, was carried on after his death in 1461 by his twenty-one-year-old son and successor Sho Toku. His problem, though, was that he rather fancied himself as a swashbuckling *wako* pirate and to no real avail, led a foolish invasion of the tiny island of Kikai in the Northern Ryukyus under the banner of the Shinto deity Hachiman, the Japanese God of War. To mark his "success" with this adventure, Sho Toku constructed a Hachiman shrine in Asato, Naha and adopted the three comma-shapes-in-a-circle insignia of Hachiman (and sea pirates) as the royal crest. However, the discontent Sho Toku thus sowed led to his downfall and early death at the age of twenty-nine.

This made way for the able administrator and former treasurer Kanemaru, who assumed kingship in 1470 under the name Sho En and founded the Second Sho Dynasty, which lasted for more than four hundred years through the following kings:

Sho En	1470–77	Sho Tei	1669–1709
Sho Seni	1477	Sho Eki	1710–12
Sho Shin	1477–1526	Sho Kei	1713–51
Sho Sei	1527–55	Sho Boku	1752–94
Sho Gen	1556–73	Sho On	1795–1802
Sho Ei	1573–88	Sho Sei	1803
Sho Nei	1589–1620	Sho Ko	1804–34
Sho Ho	1621–40	Sho Iku	1834–47
Sho Ken	1641–47	Sho Tai	1848–79
Sho Shitsu	1648–68		

Among these, Sho Shin's reign of fifty years (1477–1526)

is noteworthy because it saw many reforms and the end of the days of one-man feudalistic leadership, with a strong movement towards a centralized government with ministers and advisers. Sho Shin started his reforms by first banning the wearing of swords as personal weapons. Next, the Anji were ordered to deposit excess weapons in a warehouse at Shuri that was kept under guard. Then the Anji themselves were required to move to Shuri and take up residence near the castle, leaving administrators to look after their estates in the country. *Seppuku* (ritual suicide by disembowelment with a short sword) by faithful retainers who wished to follow their masters to death was officially banned; the castle at Shuri was elaborately decorated; the Enkaku-ji temple was built under the guidance of a Japanese priest within the castle precincts in 1492, emulating the Enkaku-ji at Kamakura, Japan; the indigenous religion was reorganized; and the Southern Ryukyus were put firmly under Okinawan control, with well-planned military expeditions and the setting up of liaison offices. However, Sho Shin's reign also saw the start of the narrowing of trade routes, as European traders gradually made headway into the area. How far-reaching Sho Shin's weapon edicts were is a matter of conjecture, as the accounts of Portuguese nationals who met Okinawan Islanders in the ports of South East Asia make frequent references to arms.

In the early 1500s Pires, one of the last Europeans to meet Ryukyuan traders in Malacca, wrote in his *Suma Oriental:*

They (the Ryukyuans) are skillful draftsmen and armorers. They manufacture gilt coffers, very rich and well-made fans, swords, (as well as) many arms of all kinds in their own style. They sail to China (from Malacca) taking merchandise that goes from Malacca to China and (then they) go on to Japan, which is an island seven or eight days' sail from there. In the said island they take (on board) gold and copper in exchange for their goods. The Ryukyuans are men who sell their merchandise freely for credit and, if they are lied to when they go to collect payment, they collect it sword in hand. Their main merchandise is gold, copper, and weapons of all kinds; (secondary merchandise consists of) coffers, boxes with gold leaf veneer, fans, and wheat—their goods are all well made. They bring a great deal of gold. They are truthful men, more so than the Chinese, and feared too. They bring (for trade) great stocks of paper and colored silks. They also bring musk, porcelain, damask, onions, and various herbs. The Ryukyuans bring swords worth thirty cruzados each and a great many of them.

Trading in weapons may have been profitable, but it did not replicate training in weapons, therefore the effectiveness of the wisdom behind Sho Shin's Weapon Edicts is questionable. Whereas his edicts protected the island from internal conflict, they left the doors wide open for external invasion. Japanese *wako* pirates had been swarming in the northern East China Sea since the thirteenth century, preying on heavily laden trade vessels like so many swarms of hornets on a lode of golden honey. Over the centuries they were gradually pushed southward and with thousands of ships, some carrying upwards of three hundred men, they audaciously began ravaging the Chinese coast, plundering whole towns and villages at a time. At their peak, the *wako* were a floating nation of criminal flotsam and jetsam and, with their headquarters at Tansui in northern Taiwan, they became a real threat to the stability of the whole Western Pacific Rim. It is probable that Portuguese accounts of Okinawans during the sixteenth century sometimes confused them with these *wako,* who would crash in on the

Okinawan traders' trusted status by passing themselves off as such.

Sometimes *wako* would travel aboard bona fide Naha-based junks and it is known that Miyako and Yaeyama Islanders were amongst the mixed nationality *wako* crews—which included Europeans and their offspring. There is also distinct evidence that *wako* had bases in the Southern Ryukyus, especially in the small, sheltered inlets on Miyako Island. Ignoring the *wako* problem only gave it free license. After 1500, junks going to and leaving Naha were sometimes preyed upon by *wako,* who later cunningly attacked villages along the Okinawan coast. The worst of these attacks occurred in 1527, when Naha itself was in danger of being ransacked. Measures were thoughtfully taken in time with the issuing of weapons from the storehouse at Shuri and the mobilization of troops. Eventually the problem became so bad, however, that between 1551 and 1553 two forts had to be built in Naha harbor as a protection against these pirate raiders. In the Orient as a whole, more technologically advanced European-style warfare was beginning to affect the traditional martial attitudes too and it is interesting to note that the first firearms to enter Japan did so through the Okinawan trading station at Tanegashima Island off Kyushu in about 1543.

Due in part to the destabilizing influence of the *wako* and the new technologies of warfare, neutral Okinawa, which had in many ways helped create the destabilization process with its lucrative, supposedly non-political arms trade, found itself more and more in the enviable position of being at the center of trade between Korea and Japan to the north, and China and Southeast Asia to the West. Okinawa had achieved this status and managed to hang on to its independence by juggling two powerful, antagonistic masters, using astute diplomatic zeal, careful political maneuvering, and a lot of kowtowing. After all, Okinawa had been a paper fief of Satsuma in Japan since 1206 and a tributary state of China since the mid-fourteenth century. But, in a way, Okinawa was wallowing in the false security of the eye of a storm of its own creation—the international intrigue it had instigated in the past for its own profit and survival through the arms trade. China and Japan could no longer trade directly with each other and both looked towards Okinawan traders to act as middlemen by moving merchandise through Naha.

Okinawan students now started to attend schools at the Five Great Temples in Japan, the same temples that had amassed great wealth from world-wide commercial ventures, and that feared the new European Catholic Christians because of the threat they posed to their power base.

In 1591, the Japanese warlord Toyotomi Hideyoshi demanded that war supplies (ten months' supply for seven thousand men) be provided by the Okinawans to help in his proposed invasion of the Asian continent, but the Ryukyuan government chose to disobey the order. The demand was repeated the following year along with a threat; the supplies were delivered promptly. Other demands were made, but nothing more was delivered. Judging from an inventory of weapons in the Shuri warehouse, drawn up in 1601 by an Okinawan official called Nago, one can see why. He lists only:

> Three hundred muskets, with one round each
> Staffs, including heavy sticks for crowd control
> Hand spears, with long, curved blades
> Hand spears, with double-edged blades
> Hand spears, with two-pronged blades
> Three hundred suits of armor, including arm
>   and shin protectors

The general lack of readily trained troops and the inaccessibility to centralized weapons stores spelt the beginning of the end for the Kingdom of Ryukyu, changing the destiny of all Okinawans, rich and poor. Toyotomi Hideyoshi's invasion plans of Asia had ended in disaster and he died in 1598. This lead to supremacy struggles in Japan that culminated in the famous battle of Sekigahara in 1600, with Tokugawa Ieyasu emerging victorious from the death and destruction. Dark intrigues followed in Japan, while in Okinawa a momentary ray of light appeared in 1603 with the introduction of a new evangelical form of Buddhism by the Japanese priest Taichu. He advocated salvation for all, regardless of caste or creed, through belief in the name of the Buddha of Infinite Life and Light, Amida.

Practical things were happening on Okinawa too, like the introduction of new foodstuffs, the sweet potato and sugar cane. But ominous clouds were gathering and lurking over the horizon; it had indeed been the calm before the storm. In 1609 intrigue had sorted itself out for awhile in Japan; Okinawa was to be the loser, the pawn. Three thousand battle-trained, professional Satsuma samurai in over one hundred junks were heading south, skirmishing among the smaller Northern islands. Their invasion of Okinawa began at Unten harbor. Okinawan inexperience and lack of military training meant slaughter and a quick defeat in the battle that followed, although Satsuma also lost many good fighting men. Limited resistance was met by the Satsuma men on the way down to Shuri, which they entered on April 5th, looting the castle and temples and exiling the king to mainland Japan for three years. Conditions of surrender were imposed, trade was controlled and taxed, and the weapon edicts were reinforced. A new chapter in the history of the Ryukyu Islands had begun.

3

Te and Kobudo Systems

In the following chapter I will detail the development of Te-based and Chinese-based Kobudo from antiquity and its relationship to Okinawan dance and religion. Naturally, the deeper one delves into history, or the past in general, the more mythical the characters who played out their roles and created the history became. More so is the case in Okinawa perhaps than in other cultures. For here reverence of the deceased as ancestral *kami* is preserved on a scale that would tend to put the Greek or Roman myths to shame. Deceased persons who played a vital role in the development of history—that in itself has become more than mythical, as exemplified in period plays and dramas—must of necessity be exonerated to godhood. All be it, in the case of those historical figures involved in the creation of Okinawan martial arts, fear of divine retribution should one not honor these gods is a major factor towards all-out deification; as is the prestige achieved from having an ancestor or a teacher who is godlike.

The deeper one delves into the history and development of Kobudo, the more Zen-like the myths may seem to be. However, in the context of the older Okinawan wishing to make a *kami* out of any and all deceased relatives or teachers, whether from fear or for prestige, by either forgiving or burying the sins that have lived after them, the unexplainable is easily explained. So let it be with Zen. The history and development of Kobudo is not a seemingly unsolvable Zen *koan* (riddle) produced from a hat by a well-meaning Buddhist priest.

Nothing is unsolvable when the right approach is used and in order to trace the origins of Te, with its related weaponry, we must approach history through the myths it has created. To demystify the myths is the course of Zen, not to propagate new ones. To purposefully make myths and create mythological beings from one's forefathers' antics and exploits on a subjective basis, thus making them into gods, is a power trip of the mightiest proportions. Why? Because the same forefather's must be, through our ancestral chains, a part our own psychic genealogical make up. They thus become us again through the karmic cycles—that is if one accepts the thought patterns of the minds that created the mythological figures in the first place. In short, by instilling a fear of the gods (the ancestral *kami*) into a population's heart and putting the same gods on an untouchable pedestal, control of that population could easily be attained without recourse to arms. Kings, nobles, priests, and martial arts teachers through the patterns of their manipulative incarnations, become untouchable reverent beings worthy of special exoneration—albeit by their own cosmic design and creation through the ages.

Nothing could be further from Zen or the true purpose of practicing Kobudo. Through the physical training involved in correct Kobudo practice and its innate, unexpressed medium that we call Zen, the body, mind, and spirit are set free. Free that is from attachment to autocratic power or imposed authority; an unseen democratic freedom that allows the amalgamation into one, thus establishing a positive dynamic force of creativity. So powerful is this force that destructive elements can simply not be. This is Zen, where myth and legend exist as mere fantasies of an era that sought to control, but in so doing destroyed itself through the destructive thought patterns it sowed in order to control. Let us therefore sift through that maze of history that surrounds Kobudo, taking its mystification with a grain of salt, yet not denying that mystification, which is after all its underlying reality—searching out, as does Zen, the objective truth within.

Motobu Seijin and the Origins of Te

Through a series of coincidental circumstances, Higa Seitoku came to purchase a parcel of land, shortly after the Second World War, at what is now the Naha City landmark of Gibo Crossroads, a busy intersection in the hills approaching Shuri. Some time later he discovered, through what is best termed psychic research, for want of a better word, that Te, or at least a Te-like martial art, had been taught at the same spot thirteen centuries earlier, in about 650 A.D. by an elderly gentleman calling himself Motobu Seijin, or Motobu the Sage. Following Motobu Seijin's "spiritual instructions" to the letter, Higa Seitoku started teaching martial arts at that very same spot and later built his dojo, the Bugeikan, there.

More psychic research revealed that Motobu Seijin had learned much of his Te-like martial art through a series of dreams and visions from three deities that appear to be part of him. He is referred to as Bugei no Kami (God, Saint, or Deity of the Martial Arts) and a portrait of him is proudly exhibited in the dojo shrine, with the following words carefully written below, "Bugei no Kami (resurrected on the twenty-first day of the eleventh lunar month, 1972), the Dragon God; on his right-hand side is the Deity of Chivalry; on his left-hand side is the venerable teacher; at his head is the martial arts teacher, Motobu Seijin (Joyous Turtle), forty-fifth generation." Higa Seitoku claims that, although he has had several earthly teachers, he has gained much of his profundity and insight of Te through a spiritual intimacy in communications with the self-same deities who taught Te to Motobu Seijin (or Bugei no Kami, The Dragon God) all those centuries ago. His teaching is, to him, "divinely inspired."

One might be inclined to consider all this hearsay but, however irrational or nonsensical such statements may appear to be, the fact is that the purported advent of Motobu Seijin in 650 A.D. is the earliest testament to a Te-like martial art having been taught on the island of Okinawa. Before disregarding such seemingly mythical explorations of history one should approach the subject from the instigator's point of view, using traditional Okinawan-style psychology to explain the thought structures of the "older" Okinawan mind, the mind that was predominant before Japanese science and computer chips affected the thought processes of the younger generations—a mere matter of translation or interpretation. First, historical fact must be considered, and from the information put forward in the previous chapter it is evident that the roots of the martial art known today as Te, along with its connected therapeutic practices and meditative Zen, probably entered the Central Ryukyuan cultural sphere, that is to say Okinawa Island, when the first civilized colonizers arrived from the Nara area of Japan in the early seventh century A.D.

These colonizers brought metal tools and weapons, notably iron ones. With such implements came the knowledge of how to use them. The more advanced the weapon or tool, the more advanced the technique of utilizing it. It is likely that the settlers would have introduced comparatively advanced bow and arrow methods, along with the hand spear and sword. Whether used in anger or not, these weapons would have represented authority, much as a holstered gun adds to the prestige of a policeman, or the possession of a siloed atomic bomb represents the ultimate, but frightening, deterrent of a technologically advanced nation. Weapon training went hand in hand with grappling and striking. A practicality, as previously noted, in case one were to lose or misplace a weapon and needed to get hold of another from one's foe.

All advanced martial art techniques must also be coordinated through meditative practices, lest they become mere empty movements or so many pretty dances. Meditation has always been part of refined martial arts practice and its incorporation into a system will distinguish such from methods that use brute force alone. So, getting back to traditional Okinawan psychology and Motobu Seijin's esoteric teacher deities, it is necessary to point out that the approximate year given, 650 A.D., is one generation after the arrival of our first civilized settlers from Japan and his "divine" teachers could have well been them (or at least their *kami*) living as ancestral deities within him. Now, as explained in Chapter One, on Okinawa the term *kami* is used to denote spirits in general; for example ancestral spirits, God, gods, deities, and saints, even holy people, are all *kami* or *kaminchu*. In fact, there is no clear distinction between the human spirit *(kami)* and deities *(kami)*. Why? Because they are one and the same. A generally held concept among persons of a sensitive or mediumistic nature on Okinawa, not easily expressed by them however, is that all *kami* once had human bodies and all bodies have a *kami*. One's higher self, or angelic nature, is the *chijigami* (head *kami*). Simplistically speaking then, the *kami* tend to pop in and out of bodies in cycles of reincarnation, as seen in the transmigration of souls.

Briefly, *kami,* using the phraseology of twentieth-century European psychology, simply means the subconscious—i.e., our spirits in traditional European thought and usually, but not always, the positive aspects thereof. A deity, such as Bugei no Kami, was once a living, breathing human being; in this case a martial arts teacher called Motobu Seijin, who would have had earthly teachers besides (or coinciding with) his divine guides, who in turn were also at one time human. Motobu Seijin passed on his art for posterity. His *kami*—his spirit, his good nature (though not all *kami* are necessarily "good"), the positive aspects of his subconscious—has now been elevated to a god-like status.

The process is a continuing one, with teachers who passed away only a few years ago being revered, at least verbally, as if they were superhuman, but who in reality had all the faults of the rest of us and were all the more human, perhaps god-like or demon-like, for it. To understand more clearly what I am getting at, the parallels between Motobu Seijin and Higa Seitoku should be looked at carefully by the reader. Then, one should take into account the similarity between the facial features of the two. When I point out that Higa Seitoku was the proud artist of the Bugei no Kami portrait displayed in the Bugeikan dojo shrine, and that it was his first attempt at such a painting, I think that the whole picture will appear to be no coincidence, but an act of creation. From the viewpoint of traditional Okinawan thought, Higa Seitoku has painted and resurrected his *kami,* his god or deity. From the viewpoint of European psychology, he has painted, using his imagination, a picture reflecting his subconscious—his mind, if you like.

Divinely inspired martial arts, to a traditional Okinawan

mind, mean the same as martial (chivalrous) arts developed through the subconscious to a modern European. The question remains, was Higa Seitoku, as he seems to suggest, once incarnate under the name Motobu Seijin in 650 A.D., following a similar pattern of life as a teacher then, as he does now? Well, maybe he did or maybe he did not, but that is a question best left for Bugei no Kami to answer, for it is his subconscious Zen riddle.

Regardless of whether or not Bugei no Kami is a figment of Higa Seitoku's imagination, or whether or not Motobu Seijin and Higa Seitoku are personages of Bugei no Kami's creation, it is my conviction that Te-like martial arts did not just happen spontaneously on Okinawa. They did not suddenly spring forth from the Ryukyuan earth. There is no connection between them and the simple Stone Age weaponry that existed before their introduction. Refined martial arts evolved from human thought processes and natural selection (survival of the fittest, strongest, and most dexterous) over many thousands of years in many different world cultures. They were affected by many individuals and circumstances, moving dynamically with the flow of history from one region to another during the passage and onslaught of Father Time.

Eventually, we see them arrive at the doorstep of the Japanese islands from the Chinese mainland via the Korean peninsula, during the Yayoi period, with the coming of the Iron Age there after 300 B.C. Once embedded in the culture, the weapons, the systems, and their thought patterns would have developed along their own lines, structured by any number of teachers, from just as many backgrounds, cultures, and philosophical schools. Ultimately they were influenced by the prevailing conditions of war and peace. Martial art development in Japan was further enhanced by the arrival of Daruma from India, his novel techniques and his Zen teachings. These concepts were perfected by Shotoku Taishi, with a distilled wisdom that straddled the civilized world and a compassion that embraced it. Finally, after combining historical documentation, tradition, myth, legend, and psychic research, we see that a highly evolved martial art probably made an appearance on Okinawa in the early seventh century with the erudite newcomers from Japan. It has been taught on the island ever since as Te.

Development of Te

During the comparatively peaceful Tenson Era on Okinawa, we can conjecture that little change in the development of Te took place for about three hundred years, until the tenth century and the construction of the first rough stone or wooden fortifications. Then, in the late twelfth century, with the Minamoto influence from Japan and later the Taira refugees fleeing from their lost battles in the north, violent changes would have occurred, typified by the murderous coup instigated by Riyu in 1187. As Okinawa adjusted to this new, brutal age and expanded its control over the outer islands, Te became a weapon for bloodlust and war; a means of making and killing enemies, rather than coming to terms with and embracing them as Daruma and Shotoku had expounded.

The strongest effects of these harsh conditions were seen during the fragmentation of the island into the Three Kingdoms in the early fourteenth century and in the hatred that division expressed. However, after the reunification of the island under Sho Hashi in 1429 and increased international trade, there would have been some positive change in Te strategy and techniques, as the system was used more and more for keeping peace rather than for starting wars. In a way, Te and its mother, Okinawa, were coming out of their own dark age. Then, a further impetus was given to the momentum of change with Sho Shin's weapon edicts in the late fifteenth century. Gradually, with the centralization of the *shizoku* at Shuri and a better legal system, Te began to transform itself back into a personal fighting art by shedding its militaristic outer skin.

There is no evidence of Chinese influence on Te during this historical era, but, when the political firepower of guns from the West came into vogue, old ideas were blown apart and the changes accelerated enormously. Man-to-man combat on the battlefield was all but dead. The final blow to Te being used as a tool of the Okinawan militarists came with the Satsuma invasion of 1609, and the massacre of the rag-tag Ryukyuan army that followed. With the removal to Japan of the remaining weapons held in storage, Ryukyu was laid bare and had little chance of ever regaining the past glory of her self-centered outward composure and any pretense of political independence. She was left naked and defenseless, leeched by the prevailing forces. The ever-present concern of the inhabitants that the tiny country was still legally claimed by China and the cold, hard facts of Satsuma's heavy taxation, control of all trade and foreign intercourse, restriction on the entry of foreigners, and reinforcement of the weapon edicts, furthered the development of diplomacy as a fine art among the Ryukyuan officials.

In this atmosphere of constant uncertainty, Te was placed at the hub of passive, non-violent intellectual protests by the Shuri upper classes. But it still offered protection to the unarmed individual against the armed *metsuke* informers planted by Satsuma. Personal bladed weapons, especially swords, were kept hidden behind closed doors as treasured family heirlooms and could not be used. Substitutes were needed for Te weapon practice; a heavy stick would stand in for a sword and a staff would become an imaginary hand spear. In case of a life-threatening situation, any available implement at hand could become a weapon of self-defense, even farm or kitchen implements and personal accessories. Organized forceful resistance of any kind, however, became as outmoded as the wearing of swords in public.

To keep the imposed harmony, hard-line supporters of a potential pro-China policy, as well as other troublesome officials, were quietly banished to the outer islands such as Miyako and Yaeyama, if lucky, or else put to death near the picturesque seashore at Koan to the north of Naha. All future kings were reduced to mere figureheads. Next, in 1669, Satsuma closed down the official swordsmithy, so that even ceremonial weapons could no longer be manufactured. By 1699, the import of all weapons was banned and demilitarization was complete. Without regular military training or wars to keep them busy, the *shizoku* at Shuri turned to such pleasurable pastimes as poetry, calligraphy, singing, dancing, horse riding, and polite conversation. The arts flourished.

Te became the highly evolved personalized martial art system for health and self-defense that we see today, possibly affected, as regards grappling, by informal exchanges of the latest techniques between Satsuma agents and Okinawan *shizoku*. Traditions of Te were passed down through certain old *shizoku* families of Shuri, surviving into the twentieth century as the "secret techniques" of several famous Karate and Kobudo masters. Like so many pieces of some unwanted archaic jigsaw puzzle, many of these Te-derived techniques were tossed upon the garbage heap of history and lost. In fact, Te, as a complete system, would have been forgotten were it not for a strange quirk of fate, perhaps divinely inspired by the foresight of a group subconscious that recognized the pearls of wisdom within it.

Te's Preservation

Such was the remarkable survival of the Motobu Udun family system of Te, a name that is apparently only coincidental to Motobu Seijin's—but then who knows? The story takes root with an Okinawan prince, Sho Koshin, the sixth son of the nondescript Ryukyuan puppet-king Sho Shitsu who reigned under Satsuma's yoke from 1648 to 1668 and died in 1688. The style of Te that Sho Koshin had inherited and improved was passed on, weapon training and all, virtually unchanged from father to eldest son down through eleven generations of his Motobu Udun family line to Motobu Choyu, who died in 1926. The Motobu Udun family had become the official Te instructors to a succession of Ryukyuan rulers and Motobu Choyu had followed suit by teaching Te to the last of the puppet kings, Sho Tai (1848–79) and his son, the Crown Prince Marquis Sho Ten.

Sho Tai reigned from 1848, remaining on the throne until 1879, the year in which Ryukyu was fully incorporated into the "enlightened" Japan of Emperor Meiji. For, in that year, the islands ceased to be a fief and became the prefecture of Okinawa; still looked down upon by Tokyo however, as a poor, rustic country cousin. Hoping to preserve his family style for posterity, Motobu Choyu opened a public dojo in 1924 at Naha with little success. His sons were not really interested in learning what were, to them, old fashioned and outmoded things, either—nor were most Okinawans, who were fighting to survive as second-class Japanese citizens in an ever-complex economic world. But a young tea boy was. Uehara Seikichi was his name and he had been a dedicated private student of Motobu Choyu for seven years, until the latter's death. Through Uehara's enthusiasm, the Motobu family style was popularized as an important intangible cultural asset and named Motobu-ryu by him in 1947, in honor of Motobu Choyu's memory. It is the oldest intact style of martial arts surviving on Okinawa today and, culturally speaking, by far the most important.

Motobu Udun Family Lineage Chart

Court Te Instructors
to a Succession of Ryukyuan Kings

King Sho Shitsu (died 1688)

Prince Sho Koshin (sixth son)	King Sho Tei (died 1709)
unknown	King Sho Eki (died 1712)
unknown	
Motobu Choko	King Sho Kei (died 1751)
Motobu Chokyu	King Sho Boku (died 1794)
unknown	King Sho On (died 1802)
unknown	King Sho Sei (died in infancy 1803)
Motobu Chosho	King Sho Ken (or Sho Ko, died 1834)
unknown	King Sho Iku (died 1847)
Motobu Chosho	King Sho Tai (1841–1901)
Motobu Choyu (died 1926)	Marquis Sho Ten (1864–1921)

Uehara Seikichi — Motobu-ryu (founded 1947)

By another stroke of good luck that almost seems to be too good to be true, the meditative aspects of Te have survived into the late twentieth century too. In fact, it seems certain that they were purposefully and with much forethought hidden away by historical figures, concealed from critical eyes in the guise of classical court dance forms, which represent another extremely important Okinawan cultural asset.

The development of dance on Okinawa is divided into three fairly distinct periods. The first and longest period was during the Ryukyu Dynastic Period, until 1879, and sees the evolution of free-form dance Te, or *Anji Kata no Me Kata* (The Dance Form of the Lords) into the stylized classical court dances. During the second period, from 1879 until the Second World War, with the advent and popularity of Karate and Kobudo from China, many new dances came into vogue. These sometimes incorporate the use of Kobudo weaponry and are made up of a series of the more robust, powerfully snappy movements of the new, fashionable fighting arts. In the third period of development, after the end of the war to the present, more creative dancing, dance forms, and choreography have become acceptable.

However, popularity of each new stage of development did not, until quite recently, change the essence and quality of the predecessors. In most instances the dances have remained as they were originally designed, although there is a tendency nowadays, on an individual basis, to put artistic expression into the postures and sometimes the faces. This trend is especially notable in the classical court dances, which initially set the foundation from which all Ryukyuan dancing has stemmed. Artistic expression in these Te martial art based dances is a modern phenomenon, reflecting the postwar era and the import of American musicals. It is of importance that none of the classical court dances incorporate weapons as such, but they do make meaningful use of ordinary, seemingly harmless, accessories such as a paper umbrella, a twig, a fan, or a hat—all of which can become weapons of defense in trained hands.

After the Satsuma invasion, several commissions *(bugyo)* were set up, one of which was for dance, i.e., dance Te, and it is not surprising that the highest Ryukyu court officials were the most accomplished dancers. Neither is it strange that, with the gradual demilitarization of the kingdom, these dance commissioners *(odori bugyo)* encouraged the choreographic interpretation of the meditative free forms of advanced Te practice into the set patterns of the court dances. In short, Te dances became secret Te katas. The deepest, most profound mysteries of Te and intrinsic energy circulation were performed to slow, relaxing music and disguised as dance, to be preserved for posterity; their treasures to be rediscovered by future generations in a more enlightened, peaceful, and realistic world. At the time, perhaps as a kind of satire, or as a means of expressing the frustration of pent-up emotions under the near-colonial Satsuma yoke, three high-ranking dignitaries from the Shuri court journeyed to the Japanese capital, boldly performing the Te-based dances before the delighted Shogun Iemitsu, with no one the wiser.

Several classical court dances from this era have been passed down unchanged to the present. Most notable of these are the Seven Women's Classical Court Dances, in which, traditionally, men dress in formal ladies' clothing to best bring out the soft female qualities of grace and gentility—dance and drama being, until after the end of the Second World War, almost entirely male domains. Nowadays however the majority of dancers, both amateur and professional, are female; modern men tend to consider such things effeminate.

The Seven Women's Classical Court Dances are as follows:

1. *Shudun* (Diverse Slow Speeds): the hand, foot, and body movements of this dance are imperceptibly slow.

2. *Inoha Bushi* (The Rhythm of Inoha [a place name]): in the dance, a young woman conceals her strong emotions behind a flower-shaped hat.

3. *Yanagi* (Weeping Willow): the tree epitomizes a Te concept, which the dance reflects—the supple branches of a weeping willow bend and flow with the wind, rather than stand against it.

4. *Amakawa* (Milky Way): a universal theme reflecting the immensity of space and the heavens.

5. *Chikuten Bushi* (Rhythm of the Rice Fields): *Chikuten* refers to the making of wet-rice paddies—a task with which the first civilized settlers are accredited.

6. *Kasekake* (The Thread Spindle): the name refers to the flat, square thread spool held by the dancer, during the dance, as if in self-defense.

7. *Motonuchibana* (Original Flower Lei): a string of red and white flowers used in the dance represents tenderness.

The most popular of all the formal classical court dances is *Kajadefu,* also called *Gozenfu* (Before the Lord), which has of late been classed as a *Rojin no Odori* (Old People's Dance). Originally, the dance was performed by those of all ages as part of ceremonies welcoming foreign dignitaries. It represents the spirit of longevity and bountifulness.

In context, but not form or technique, the Okinawan classical court dances resemble the slow-moving, meditatively dynamic concepts of the well-known Chinese Boxing system Taijiquan. Furthermore, the themes of intrinsic energy flow are the same between the two. Likewise, teaching expressions used in Te training, such as, "feel as if the head is held up by an invisible, fine thread," or, "hold the arms and hands as if water is gently running off them," are similar to those used in Taijiquan instruction. Also, like Taijiquan, each Te-dance movement has a specific name; for example "Throw Hand" and "Watching the Moon Hand." Both systems refrain from double weighting, in that, except at the beginning or end of a series of movements, most of the body weight is moved from one leg to the other in a fluid manner. While dancing, the body weight is never dispersed equally between the two feet.

Where the two systems differ is in the actual hand-and-foot movements, and thus in technique, too. The Te-based classical court dances appear more sedate to the eye and they do not have long stances nor does Taijiquan have the stretching-out arm movements that are common in basic Te. Also unlike Taijiquan, which tends more to the horizontal, there are rising-up movements on the toes (following the high musical notes), as well as sinking-down movements (with the lower notes) that correspond to Te grappling technique. In Te-based dances, the spine is held straight and, usually, erect, and the overall style provides no opening for an imaginary attacker.

The last and by far the most well known of the Ryukyuan dance commissioners was Tamagusuku Chokun, who lived from 1684 to 1738. His name is a household word in Okinawa, especially in the Shuri area. In 1718, at the age of 35, he became the dance commissioner for the second time by popular decision. The dictates of propriety, despite his obvious genius, disqualified him the first time round because he was considered too young for the post by some of the older authorities. He is best remembered for his five operatic dance-dramas *(kumi odori)*, a collection of dramatized stories from various Okinawan villages that present diverse themes such as vendetta and filial piety. They are mostly derived from the Three Kingdoms Era, being choreographic enactments of historical or legendary events that were performed annually at village festivals, rather like the nativity plays held in Western churches at Christmas time. Chokun Tamagusuku is credited with putting the plays together over a four to five year period; the first two, *Nido Tekiuchi* and *Shushin Kaneiri* having premiered in 1719 before visiting Satsuma officials. The only problem he had, reportedly, was translating the Shuri dialect into contemporary Japanese.

Nido Tekiuchi (Two Sons' Revenge), popularly known as *Gosamaru Tekiuchi* (Gosamaru Vendetta), is about two youths who avenge the death of their father, Gosamaru at the cunning hands of Amawari (see page 84). In *Shushin Kaneiri* (Devotion Inside a Bell), a vindictive young man, *Nakagusuku Wakamachi* (Young Pine of Nakagusuku), hides his spirit, along with his nasty emotions, inside a large bronze Buddhist temple bell at Shuri. During the reigns of King Sho Boku (1752–94) and King Sho On (1795–1802), Tamagusuku's plays were still popular with visiting Satsuma officials. Records show that his other plays were shown at this time. For example there was *Koko no Maki* (A Tale of Filial Piety), a fable about respect for one's parents, and *Onna Monoguri* (Crazy Woman), a ghost story about the frenzied soul of a dead woman who, because she hung on to her bitter emotions, could not rise to Heaven.

The last of the five dramas was titled *Tennyo Monogatari* (The Story of a Heavenly Maiden) or *Mikaru Shi* (Child of Mikaru), which tells of a beautiful woman who came down from Heaven, but who had her golden feathered cloak stolen by a man while she was bathing in a sacred spring, and therefore could not go home. Unwillingly, she had to marry him and bear his children before she could get her cloak back and return to Paradise. Near Ojana in central Okinawa there is a cool, crystal-clear spring and tree-shaded sacred grove thought to be the historical place where the roots of this myth took hold. In the story, *Hagaromo Densetsu* (Legend of the Feathered Cloak), still told today, the naughty man who hid the feathered garment about 650 years ago was called Okuma and our reluctant Heavenly Maiden bore him a boy and a girl. All's well that ends well though, because the boy grew up to marry a daughter of the then-Lord of Katsuren Castle and went on to become Lord of Urasoe. At the age of thirty, he was king of Central Okinawa, encouraging trade and cultural exchange with China. Of course he is better known as Satto, King of Chuzan from 1350 to 1395.

When the irrelevant (to a martial artist) external trappings of traditional overdress and more recent exaggerated showy movements (that have grown out of a need for outward artistic self-expression among the younger novice dancers) are stripped away, the classical court dances as performed by the top professionals provide us with a living museum piece of advanced Te—a showcase of ancient wisdom ready to be reawakened. What has been preserved from generation to generation within the dances, are breath control for amalgamating the body, mind, and spirit, linked with the vibrant, all-but-concealed, internal utilization of intrinsic energies—utilization from within to help others without. Martial artists from the Western world schooled in the internal Chinese Boxing systems of Taiji, Xingyi, Bagua, or soft versions of Shaolin Temple boxing, refer to this as *qigong*, exercising the *qi* (*ki* in Japanese), the intrinsic energy. For the serious, long-term martial artist, this internal "spiritual" training of the subconscious is the epitome, the very embodiment of his or her art, obtained after constant, arduous effort. In European culture and phraseology, its knowledge is known as spiritual awareness, or mind over matter. On Okinawa, its practice is not an intellectual pastime talked about over cups of tea, but an "unsaid" way, often unknowingly, of achieving Zen in action.

From beginning to end, the five operatic dance-dramas left to us by Tamagusuku Chokun contain all the essence of the classical court dances. As a whole, they are a complete meditative process unto themselves and should not be looked upon merely, from a martial artist's point of view, for their role in having preserved the realistic fighting strategies of the times in their splendidly detailed fighting scenes. More than a time capsule of Te strategy in motion, they provide us with the means of regulating the voice with the breath (the voice being a reflection of the soul), through harmonic singing and chant-like poetic sequences. They provide an insight into the *"kami* psychology" of a past group-subconscious mind of a highly sophisticated nation. A past mind that, under differing terminology, straddles the ages. What were mere musical plays for entertainment, to the comparatively brusque Satsuma officials, were the condensed esoteric expression of Te that survived on Okinawa through its own weeping-willow strategy, aided by the very power that sought to destroy it.

The classical court dances, the operatic dance-dramas, or period plays, as they stand in the late twentieth century, besides their aesthetic appeal are, at their roots, a magnificent reflection of that bygone epoch, waiting to be rediscovered for their true worth and potential. Such are the eternal truths, the "mysteries" of Zen.

Arrival of Chinese-based Kobudo

By the early 1700s, the population of the Okinawan *shizoku* upper classes, who had been required to live at Shuri, had far outstripped its worth. With international trade dwindling and profits being creamed off by greedy Satsuma, the subsequent pressure on resources, along with a need for increased food production, meant more freedoms regarding choice of profession being granted to them without loss of rank. From the 1720s on, many seized opportunity and took to manufacturing luxury goods, starting transportation businesses, or managing farms. While the eldest sons would carry on with their traditions of higher education, often abroad, and retain the pampered Shuri lifestyle, many a younger son found it more profitable to raise cash crops on their old family estates in the country-side. They established pioneer farming communities, or lived as country squires on the parceled-out tracts of land, which they were eventually able to buy or sell for profit.

One of these new settlements that grew up from the farming communities was the village of Tancha in Northern Okinawa. Near the center of the village is a tiny red-tiled shrine dedicated to the deity Guandi (Wudi), the Chinese patron of military affairs and personnel. He became ro-manticized as an army commander and a sort of Chinese Robin Hood figure during the Chinese age of chivalry in their Three Kingdoms era of the third century A.D. In reality, though, he was executed in 219 after rescuing a maiden in distress from the clutches of a nasty magistrate. He is usually pictured (as at the Tancha shrine) sitting next to his young son with a fierce looking squire standing beside him holding a protective Chinese glaive.

In 1594 Guandi was canonized by a Ming dynasty em-peror as the country's god of war, becoming protector of China and its entire population. Thousands of his *Wu–shengmiao* (Sacred Warrior Temples and Shrines) sprang up all over the country and in the seventeenth century Guan-di's cult had spread to Korea, where it was widely believed that it was his spirit that had saved the country from inva-sion by the Japanese. He was particularly revered by every-day folk due to the belief that he had an uncanny power over demonic beings. In the reign of Qianlong (1735–96), at the height of Chinese enthusiasm for Guandi, a Chinese envoy visiting Okinawa strongly urged the Ryukyuan king and his ministers to build a temple at Naha. The deity has been revered in certain areas of Okinawa ever since.

(Detail) Guandi (center) with his son (right) and a squire (left).

Guandi's strong association with weaponry is displayed inside the Tancha shrine; next to a portrait of the thousand-armed Kannon (with a thousand weapons) Avalokitesvara, are two pairs of mock-up weapons (two swords and two glaives). The originals were destroyed, bartered for, or taken as war souvenirs during the Battle of Okinawa in 1945, along with hundreds of others from similar shrines.

Following in the spiritual footsteps of the cult of Guandi came a surge of interest in Chinese martial arts. Although restrictions on travel, foreign intercourse, the import of weapons, and weapon training remained tight, throughout most of the eighteenth and nineteenth centuries Okinawans have been recorded as having visited or lived in China for the express purpose of studying the martial arts. On returning to Okinawa thcy brought back new hand-held weapons and the means of using them. Most of these Shaolin-based Chinese systems continued evolving in technique and kata, surviving into the twentieth century in a number of individual systems that are collectively referred to as Kobudo. There has been a definite parallel development of these styles on Okinawa, alongside the introduction and development of Shaolin-derived Karate from the Fuzhou area.

This was especially so in the late eighteenth or early nineteenth century with the introduction of the first empty-hand (Karate) kata, called Kusanku, by a Chinese master of the same name. It is these Chinese Shaolin roots, that show up in stances, technique, terminology, and kata of Chinese-based Kobudo and Karate that clearly differentiate them, as a grouping, from Te weapons training; the roots of which were introduced from Japan much earlier. Kobudo and Te, although they both have similar origins tracing back to Daruma and his Zen have evolved technically in their own separate ways. They are two distinct combat arts; two sons sired by one father, nurtured in separate wombs. Both however have one esoteric aim, the development of body, mind, and spirit.

Tradition in the Motobu peninsula holds that some time after the Satsuma invasion of 1609, several locals with family roots growing back to Shuri, ran away for reasons unknown to the newly founded Fuzhou branch of the Shaolin

Temple, where they learned the use of the staff and other weapons. There they remained, the story goes, for about ten years. On returning to Okinawa they went back to farming and changed the weapon katas they had learned into dances, to thrill the audiences at the regular festivals.

Typically, the exact date of this escapade is not given, however, as the Motobu farmers in question are described as having been descendants of *shizoku* families, they could only have settled in Motobu after the 1720s. A minimum of at least one generation should be added to this time reference point, therefore, to give a reasonable date for their stay at the Shaolin temple, placing it sometime between the mid-eighteenth and early nineteenth centuries. In the twentieth century, several of the still-surviving popular weapon dances were readapted back into katas for weapon training by a number of teachers, a trend that is seen not only on the Motobu Peninsula but all over Okinawa. These katas nowadays form the basis of such Kobudo styles as Honshin-ryu, founded by Miyagi Masakazu at Toguchi on the Motobu Peninsula in about 1975.

Matsuda of Henachi hamlet was another Motobu farmer who journeyed to China to learn martial arts, this time in the late nineteenth century. He brought back with him the use of the heavy Chinese glaive, the techniques of which survive on Okinawa as part of the Karate (and Kobudo) style known as Mabuni Kenwa Shito-ryu. This style was founded in 1948 by a Karate teacher called Uechi Kanyei, who was born into a family at Untenbaru in Motobu and learned the use of the Chinese glaive from his uncle and grandfather as part of his family martial arts system. Like so many families in the area, they were descendants of *shizoku* who had migrated from Shuri.

One of the most prominent families to have formulated a Shaolin-based Kobudo and Karate style is known by the name Kojo. Originally, though, the family bore the Chinese name Sai, because they were descended from one of the "Thirty-Six Families" of Chinese artisan immigrants who settled at Kume village, Naha way back in 1393, under the guidance of King Satto. Even after five hundred years, they kept their educational and cultural ties with China, only losing their distinct Chinese identity in the twentieth century. The mold of the family fighting system was set by Kojo Uekata (or Sai Ko), who studied weaponry and a grappling art in China sometime in the mid-eighteenth century and who passed his techniques on to his sons. One of these was Kojo Pechin who was nicknamed Nmari Bushi (Born Knight). He further honed his father's teaching techniques into the fundamentals of the family style in the late eighteenth century.

Kojo Uekata's grandson, Sai Shoi (1816–1906), referred to in his mature years as Seijin Tanmei (Wise Old Man, or Sage), further studied Chinese weaponry, including the stick, at Fuzhou and taught sword- and knife-concealment techniques along with the use of the staff to male members of his family. In 1848, at the age of sixteen, Sai Shoi's son Kojo Isei (1832–91) learned Chinese weaponry at Fuzhou with his cousin, Kojo Taitei (1837–1917) from a Chinese military attaché named Iwah, who is known to have made visits to Okinawa. Eventually, they both came to be noted for skill in archery and the use of the hand spear. Taitei, also known as Goken Tanmei (Hard-fisted Old Man), also learned Chinese Boxing from a teacher called Wanxinxiang and managed to smuggle back some weapons from China but these were lost during the Battle of Okinawa, like so many other historically valuable treasures and artifacts.

Next in the Kojo family line comes Kojo Kaho (1849–1925), who grew up in his father's absence at Kume village, which was still looked upon as being the old erudite Chinese quarter, the Chinatown of the Naha-Shuri area. After one of his trips to Okinawa, Iwah took the promising lad Kaho back to Fuzhou and taught him Chinese Boxing. On gaining his teaching credentials, he opened a dojo in Fuzhou that became quite well known among the long-established expatriate community of Okinawans, some of whom are recorded as having trained there. The use of the stick was reintroduced into the Kojo family fighting system at this time, along with an important stick kata that is still extant. Following in his father, Kaho's, footsteps, Kojo Saikyo (1873–1941), learned the family fighting art and passed it, along with the use of the staff and stick, to his son Kafu, who was born in 1909.

Kojo Kafu also trained under his grandfather and uncle Kojo Shuren and, after the war, decided to go commercial again by starting a dojo in Naha and calling his style Kojo-ryu. Although composed mostly of empty-hand Karate techniques with much Chinese-based arm and wrist grappling, Kojo-ryu includes the use of the stick and staff with their respective katas. Unfortunately though, because Kojo Kafu prefers a quiet and peaceful retired life in the green Southern Okinawan countryside to the noise and pollution of Naha City, the style is not taught on the island at present.

During the nineteenth century there were other notable Okinawans studying Kobudo and related fighting arts abroad. Sakugawa Satunushi, who hailed from Akata Village in Shuri, was most noteworthy among these, having learned the use of the staff and other weapons in China. Appropriately, his nickname, "Tode" Sakugawa, was bestowed on him because of his skill at Chinese Boxing (Tode), which he had learned from the Chinese master Kusanku. In the mid-nineteenth century, Sakugawa taught the use of weapons to Chinen Pechin (or, Yamagusuku Andaya), who passed them on to his son Sanda (alias Yamani, or Yamane Tanmei). Chinen also learned much from a relative called Chinen Shichiyanaka and, together with his son, Chinen Masami (1898–1976), a former policeman in colonial Taiwan, put together a representative set of festival dance katas from all over Okinawa and devised, with the incorporation of a few Te techniques, the Kobudo style Yamani-ryu. The title was taken from an old family name, but the style ceased to exist on the death of Chinen Masami in 1976.

However, many of the Yamani-ryu staff katas are preserved as part of the weapon training curricula of the Bugeikan, Ryukyu Kobudo, and the Shorin-ryu Karate style of the teacher Nakazato Shugoro. "Tode" Sakugawa also taught staff; and possibly his Karate techniques, to the Okinawan master, "Bushi" Matsumura Sokon (c.1809–1901), who was the originator of what is nowadays referred to as the "Shorin" group of Karate styles, considered synonymous with Shuri-te (or -de); the Chinese-based Tode (Karate), that later developed at Shuri. Even so, only about half of the Shorin styles include weapon practice as a main part of their curriculums. Matsumura and others of his vintage learned Chinese Boxing under Iwah, as well as another Chinese military attaché named Ason, but to what extent the latter two instructed Okinawans in weaponry has not been fully ascertained.

What is known, though, is that Matsumura journeyed to Fuzhou twice on official business and it is said that he visited the Shaolin Temple, but what weapon techniques or katas he picked up there have not been recorded. On a one-time trip to Satsuma, he is believed to have been coached in the use of the sword by the Japanese Yashichiro Ijuin of Jigen-ryu Ken-jutsu. As a long-serving bodyguard and probably Tode instructor to the last three successive

Ryukyuan kings, Sho Ken, Sho Iku, and Sho Tai, Matsumura Sokon's influence on the development of Kobudo was outstanding, having passed his forms down either directly or indirectly through the following teachers: Matsumura Nabe, Kanagusuku Sanda, Tokumine Pechin, Gushikawa Tiragwa, Tawata Pechin, and Chinen Shichiyanaka's teacher, Soeishi.

Matsumura Nabe, grandson of Matsumura Sokon, passed on the style to the Karate teacher Soken Hohan, who founded his own style Matsumura Orthodox Shorin-ryu, in 1952, which includes staff katas and the use of the sickle. Kanagusuku Sanda (AKA Kinjo Uhuchiku) taught *sai* techniques to Kina Shosei who in turn passed these on to several Okinawans, including Isa Shinyu, the creator of Uhuchiku Kobudo. Tokumine Pechin passed his Kobudo knowledge indirectly to the Karate teacher Kyan Chotoku (1870–1945) and the essence remains today preserved as a staff kata, Tokumine no Kun, in the Karate style Shorinji-ryu that was founded by a schoolteacher, Nakazato Shugoro, on the Chinen Peninsula in 1947—the same staff kata is also to be found in Okinawa Kenpo, which was formulated by Nakamura Shigeru (c.1892–1969) and named as such after the war. Gushikawa Tiragwa's Kobudo affected the development of the (mainly) Karate styles Shorin-ryu, Ryukyu Shorin-ryu, and Matayoshi Kobudo. The teachings of Tawata Pechin are preserved in Ryukyu Kobudo.

Another culturally important import from China to Okinawa was the Shaolin-based weapon and Chinese Boxing system that was taught at Fuzhou by a Chinese master named Ru Ru Ko. In the latter half of the nineteenth century, a young man named Nakaima Norisato (c. 1850–1927), whose official name was Nakaima Pechin and who was another Kume village local, went to Fuzhou, China for long-term overseas studies. While there he was introduced to Ru Ru Ko by the retired military attaché known as Goei and had time to learn much of the former's teaching of weaponry and *heiho* (military tactics). After five or six years of arduous practice, Nakaima received a certificate stating that he had mastered the history of armaments, distribution of provisions, ways of instructing troops, military maneuvers, ways of attacking and subduing, etc., and had progressed well in his training.

Before returning to Okinawa, he was able to travel around the Fujian, Guangzhou, and Beijing areas collecting all kinds of weaponry, some of which he managed to bring back with him. His fighting arts were passed on down through his son, Nakaima Kenchu, to his grandson Kenko who, going against his better judgment, broke his family pledge of secrecy and started to teach the style on a public basis in 1971 to a group of about twenty schoolteachers. For a name,

Shorin-ryu karate training at Nakazato Shugoro's dojo in Naha.

he chose Ryuei-ryu and, although primarily a Karate style, it includes the use of fourteen "Chinese weapons": namely, *sai, kama, renkuan, tinbe, gekiguan, kon, bisento, yari, tonfa, suruchin, dajio, nunchaku, tankon,* and *gusan.*

There were other Okinawans who made the trip to Fuzhou to study under Ru Ru Ko, one of whom was Sakiyama Kitoku, a "brother disciple" of Nakaima Norisato in China and teacher of Kuniyoshi Shinkichi back on Okinawa. By the late nineteenth century, about ten years after Nakaima Norisato first arrived at Ru Ru Ko's school, another Okinawan, Higaonna Kanryo (1853–1917), had found his way to the door. He had arrived there at the age of twenty-four and it seems, due to Ru Ru Ko's advanced years, was influenced more by the younger, then chief instructor, Wanxinxiang. Not much is known of him, but under the name Wansu (or Wan Shu), Wanxinxiang is thought to have been in Okinawa with Matsumura Sokon's teacher, the military attaché Ason who during his sojourn, it is believed, directly instructed Sakiyama, Gushikawa Tiragwa (AKA Gushi), and Tomoyore.

On returning to Okinawa himself, Higaonna instructed, among others, Miyagi Chojun, who in 1937 (unofficially) started his weaponless "hard-soft" Karate style, Goju-ryu—a style that was heavily influenced by the Fujian White Crane of a Chinese tea dealer, Gokenki (1886–1940), who lived in Naha and traveled to Fuzhou with Miyagi in 1915 on a disappointing research trip, or quest, in search of Wanxinxiang and the lost Ru Ru Ko school. Like Higaonna, Uechi Kanbun (1877–1948) made the trip to Fuzhou and learned an interesting derivative (or sister style) of Ru Ru Ko's system that, on Okinawa, formed the basis of the popular Karate style Uechi-ryu, which he created after the Second World War.

The new styles of Karate and, to a lesser extent Kobudo,

that were derived from Ru Ru Ko's and Wanxinxiang's teachings, grew up in Naha to be known popularly as Naha-te; the Tode of Naha. Similarly, Tomari-te, the Tode of Tomari Village, the old port of Naha, was derived from the teachings of a Chinese castaway called Anan, who taught his brand of Chinese Boxing to some locals there in the middle or late nineteenth century. Tangible proof that Chinese weaponry and its related Boxing systems were becoming popular with fashionable young males during the late eighteenth and nineteenth centuries is recorded in a number of documents. A turn-of-the-century scroll painting by the artist Shiba Kokan (1738–1818), appropriately labeled "Bachelor's Party," shows a scene of rampant debauchery in which a drunken macho male is challenging to a fight another male, who is draped around a geisha in a defensive Te-like pose. The challenger is clearly demonstrating the latest, contemporary Kusanku-style Chinese-boxing tactics.

Surviving pictorial scenes of the Ryukyuan Parade of Investiture to Edo (Tokyo) in the 1830s cast light on an almost carnival sort of atmosphere, with Okinawans, dressed in their finest clothes, carrying great ceremonial weapons of office (especially the pronged glaive of Guandi fame, and the forked hand spear or arrow), of Chinese design. Living historic flashes from this era are still recreated every year in the annual Shuri Festival, with young men reenacting the parade by carrying wooden mock-ups of the same weapons. At the Higashionna library at Yogi Park in Naha is a rare nineteenth century-booklet that would appear to be the collected notes, or report, of one Watanabe Keiho, who studied weaponry and military arts in China. Although this carefully, hand-written textbook lists the use of the sword, hand spear, and bow and arrow with Chinese techniques, it also indicates the ever-increasing importance of firearms by including detailed scale drawings of guns.

Indeed, in 1853, with the arrival of the American Commodore Perry and his "Black Ships" in Naha harbor (on his way to force open the gates of Japan) and his show of arms to gain entry to Shuri castle, Okinawans were in a quandary as to how to defend themselves against aggression on a personal as well as a governmental level. In fact the problem was highlighted all through the nineteenth century by observant European and American artists who astutely depicted the carrying of arms (both guns as well as swords) on Okinawa by foreign dignitaries and Satsuma officials, whereas the Okinawans are always shown bearing little more than paper fans, sunshades, and long pipes. These "accessories" were among the seemingly frail, secret armory of weapons adopted by a politically subjected and erudite upper class; people who were psychologically strong yet for the sake of survival had to appear to be physically weak. Their strength was in their meekness.

Times were changing rapidly, though. An informative Japanese book, *Nanto Zatsuwa,* published around 1880, gives a somewhat biased pictorial and written account of life among the everyday people of Okinawa as they adjusted to the new, classless Japanese society of the post-Meiji Restoration era. It is interesting to see cartoons of Ryukyuan Islanders hunting wild boars with weapons such as the glaive, heavy stick, and musket that had been passed down for generations as family heirlooms. Strangely, the book includes a detailed sketch of three Satsuma men visiting a wealthy Okinawan house; times had not changed completely, it would seem, because their thoughtfully placed sheathed swords are an obviously potent display of post-colonial authority and intimidation. In the book, behavioral patterns are recorded, sometimes mistakenly, in that the author notes that many Okinawans with upper-class *bushi* (Okinawan samurai, or *shizoku*) surnames had taken to drinking and fighting—some even to begging in the streets. What he had unknowingly witnessed, no doubt, were proud displays of Kobudo and Karate performed eagerly by medicine hawkers as a part of their street advertising campaigns. These shows of seemingly magical strength were, in a way, the precursors of the spectacular Karate demonstrations one sees world-wide today.

One of the most fascinating facts recorded in *Nanto Zatsuwa* was the then-extant use and practice of the musket and bow and arrow as historic martial arts by the "Southern Island Kawasaki family," who had inherited the techniques from their grandfather. Where these arts originated from is not known, nor is it known where they disappeared to—they have vanished from the islands without a trace, to be replaced by Olympic-style shooting and Japanese sport archery, or *kyudo*. Towards the end of the 1800s, *The Takanoya Account of Okinawan Culture,* which was first published in June 1896, mentions that blank shots were often heard to ring out at tug-of-war festivals on Okinawa and the magazine records how at one such festival, six young men dressed as Okinawan samurai, "with golden turbans," beat against each other's white canes in time to music. In another stick dance, three children receive golden canes from the orchestra to hit with and, in yet another, four children carry three-foot sticks with a flower tied to each end. During practice for the tug-of-war, slow or lazy boys were lightly coaxed with the aid of a straw rope and village elders would teach the boys how to "wrestle with hands and sticks or by pushing bodies." Six-foot staffs were used to support the massive, rice-straw rope—a sight that is still commonplace at the Naha tug-of-war held yearly on Kokusai Dori (International Street).

4

The Modern Kobudo Scene

Moving away from the nineteenth and into the twentieth century, the momentum of the introduction of new weapon-based fighting arts into Okinawa did not cease, despite the harm done to Chinese Boxing during the Boxer Rebellion of 1900. This was an uprising, under the banner of the dragon, against technological progress, Christians, and the foreign community, by martial artists organized into secret societies who found out the hard way that their art was not magical and their bodies were not hardened enough to be impervious to modern bullets. Invariably, some of the lucky ones who survived and fled the aftermath, ended up on Taiwanese as well as Okinawan shores.

Some years later, a Naha-born Okinawan, going by the name Matayoshi Shinko (1888–1947), managed to travel to China twice. In about 1911, he crossed from Hokkaido (the northern island of Japan proper) to Manchuria, where he stayed for a couple of years and got in league with a gang of mounted bandits. His second trip took him to Fuzhou and Shanghai; it was a little less adventurous and he returned in 1934. Before his death in 1947, Matayoshi Shinko was able to pass on most of his hard-earned knowledge to his son Shinpo, who established the Ryukyu Kobudo Federation in 1970, after having opened a school for Kobudo instruction at Naha in 1969. This almost exclusively weapon-based style had already influenced the Kobudo of the Goju-ryu Karate teacher Higa Seiko in his formulation of Kokusai Kobudo in 1958 and, much later, was the style of Kobudo adopted by the founders of Pangai-noon-ryu, an old name for a new hybrid derived from the Okinawan Karate style Uechi-ryu.

The prewar years had seen numerous Okinawans posted to the growing colonies of Taiwan, Korea, and Manchuria as administrators, soldiers, engineers, or pioneer farmers. For those who had a background knowledge of martial arts and were sent to Taiwan, it was a field day. Among such were three former government employees. One of them was a policeman, Chinen Masami of Yamani-ryu fame, who learned the use of the *sai* there, along with other weapons, but, due to the allied terms of surrender, he was not permitted to return with the real articles and subsequently left them at a temple near Tainan City. Another of the three was Ishikawa Horoku, a schoolteacher and postwar founder of the Karate style Shiroma Shinpan Shito-ryu, who had known Chinen Masami in Tainan and was related to him—he too did research into Chinese Boxing.

The last, but by no means least of the three was the former senior civil servant, Kinjo Eiji (1899–1995), a close relative of mine by marriage and a martial artist par excellence. A highly educated man and would-be philosopher of note, with an open, yet obscure, sense of humor that would often incense the recipient before one had time to fathom the complex depth of the joke. He, to me, was Zen; the personification of it in a teacher. Although in the proud position of being the eldest son of an eldest son, Kinjo Eiji would not have any of this "superficial 'Sensei' stuff" and preferred to be called by his nickname, Saburo (a name usually reserved for happy-go-lucky third sons), writing the middle syllable *bu* with the same Chinese character as the *bu* in *kobudo, bushi, bugei,* and *bukyo* (chivalry).

Maturing as a young man in Ishimine, Shuri, he had mastered his family's Te grappling and pressure-point therapy system, along with stick defense and sword by his late twenties, in addition to hard training in Tode under several of the teachers who were popular at the time in Shuri and Naha.

Living and working abroad enabled him to further his martial arts studies by taking up Taijiquan (especially the sword), as well as, "a bit of Fujian Shaolin Quan," for which he received certification as a master. After the war, he was "too busy and too tired" to teach Tigwa (Te and related arts) and it took a good deal of convincing from myself and other relatives at family reunions to persuade him to pass on his knowledge. In the early 1980s we came up with the idea of naming his style and, after long deliberation, finally decided that Ryukyu Bugei (Ryukyuan Martial Arts) would be the most appropriate title. Later, in 1989, to commemorate the publication of my book, *Okinawan Karate: Teachers, Styles & Secret Techniques,* which Kinjo Eiji had helped me with immensely, we combined the essence of what I had learned from other teachers with his brilliance and experience to form *Sogo Bugei no Kai* (Universal Martial Arts Federation), the aim being to incorporate martial arts from differing cultural backgrounds into an all-inclusive and comprehensive system with health and self-development as its primary objective.

One of the major reasons for the spread of Kobudo, along with Karate, to the Japanese mainland in the 1920s and 1930s had been its recommendation to the powers that were, following a letter to the Okinawan Prefectural Education Department in 1908 by an influential Okinawan, an ex-court secretary and Tode teacher from Shuri, Itosu Anko (1832–1916), who had learned Tode from the famous Matsumura Sokon. Itosu thought that Tode would be an excellent means of personal discipline and self-defense for officers and men on the battlefield—little could his forceful character have envisaged their fateful end. To obscure the Chinese roots of Kobu-jutsu and Tode for Japanese militarists in the 1920s, the truth was distorted and Tode (Chinese Boxing) became Karate (empty hands). It was at this time also that Kobu-jutsu began to be called Kobudo, giving it a more sporty appeal.

The person who unwittingly found himself spearheading the introduction of Karate to Japan in 1922 was Itosu Anko's student Funakoshi Gichin (1868–1957), a humble schoolteacher and founder in Japan of the highly popular sport Karate style Shotokan, which first brought the art world recognition in the decades after the war. Following suit, Okinawan Kobudo was introduced to the Japanese mainland at about the same time, by the likes of such men as Yabiku Moden (1882–c.1945), another student of Itosu Anko, who had trained in weaponry under Chinen Sanda, Tawata Pechin, and *sai* expert Kanagusuku Sanda. Unlike Karate development in Japan though, Kobudo was not generally subject to the presently outlawed, sadistic *shigoki* death drilling one saw (and still unfortunately sees) in mainland Japanese university clubs. Its standard of training has remained comparatively unscathed by the process of early twentieth-century autocratic militarization.

Devastation was all that was left of Okinawa Island after the air raids on the Naha-Shuri area in 1944 and the Battle of Okinawa that started on Easter morning April 1, 1945— perhaps, one could cruelly envision, as some sort of retaliatory April Fool. Armageddon was let loose relentlessly for nearly three solid months as the bombs rained down indiscriminately and a one-time "paradise island" was churned into a living hell. Okinawa and its populace were once again an unfortunate party in a battle of superpower wills. Both primitive and high-tech weaponry had taken their toll but, on the bright side, most of the population survived, protected, as it were, in reverse by the forward projection of karma from their ancestors. The same dead ancestors who, when living, had provided them with excellent air raid shelters—the ancient stone family tombs.

In the aftermath of this outsiders' war, Shuri and Naha were reduced to a rubble-strewn land of lost dreams. Out of their ashes, though, the phoenix was already rising, as postwar reconstruction was set in motion under the experienced direction of the U.S. military. The process accelerated after reversion to Japan in 1972, and Okinawa Prefecture was catapulted back into the forefront of the industrial age. This period of postwar renewal saw an unprecedented overhaul of society from bottom to top. The ruins of Shuri castle, the one-time pride of Ryukyu, for example, was quarried for its rubble to build the grand north-south American-style Highway no. 1. Then parts of the castle were tastefully restored and the whole area turned into the central seat of learning in the prefecture, with the building of the University of the Ryukyus, funded in part by money donated from the U.S. In the 1980s the ugly stone multistory university buildings were pulled down with a plan to fully restore the castle to its former glory and open it up as a public park by the turn of the millennium.

The popularity of martial arts was given a boost due to the perceived commercial benefits, as young Okinawan men and women eased their sense of insecurity at being host to several thousand U.S. service personnel stationed on the prefecture's extensive network of bases. It was also during

Taira Shinken.

this time that Okinawan Kobudo, following in the footsteps of Karate, started to spread to North America, Eu-
rope, and beyond, mostly due to military personnel who
learned the fighting arts off base, or at one of the camps
such as Camp Hansen, a major U.S. marine training base
for jungle warfare. This international climate of recognition paved the way for such well-known Kobudo teachers
as Chinen Kenyu being invited to teach in France, along
with Iha Koei in Germany and Oshiro Zenyei in Spain.

The noted Kobudo teacher Taira Shinken had given extra prestige to Kobudo on Okinawa in the late 1950s by
publishing *Ryukyu Kobudo Taiken,* the first comprehensive
book in Japanese on the subject. Chinese Boxing and weaponry continued to influence the development of Karate and

Kobudo in the postwar era, with the introduction of Bagua from Taiwan in 1973 by Kinjo Akio, an Okinawan karate-ka who trained under Kinryu, "The Golden Dragon," in Taiwan. He teaches Bagua on the island of Miyako, along with Chinese weaponry. A Taijiquan-like fighting art was practiced on Okinawa before the war at Itoman in the south of the island, by an obscure Okinawan *bushi* called Machiya Buntoku (AKA Kinjo Matsu—for in Okinawa, Kinjo is to Jones, as Higa is to Smith) who had trained in Fuzhou. His art was scoffed at, though, and has not survived.

With the relaxation of China's borders in the 1970s and 1980s, a gentleman, Mr. China (pronounced "Cheena"), from Shuri was able to spend several years and a sizable fortune learning internal Chinese Boxing and weaponry from the villages around Fujian Province. On returning to Okinawa, following the world trend towards the "soft" martial arts, he started teaching his Taikyokuken Tode (Taijiquan Karate) inclusive of Taijiquan sword and other weaponry at a sports center in Furujima near Naha, as well as at his dojo in Ojana, Central Okinawa. Needless to say, he soon accumulated a large following of students.

In 1963, with the publication of his Japanese and English language book, *Dance of Ryukyu and Self Defense Dances,* an attempt was made by the dance choreographer and teacher Yamanouchi Seihin to combine Kobudo and Karate movements with music. The result is what Yamanouchi called "self-defense dances" examples of which were "Rhythm-Karate," "Rhythm-Sai, and "Rhythm-Haku-tsuru" (White Crane). He also included "Mekata," which he defined as, "dances with Karate techniques imposed here and there, or Karate adjusted freely to the tempo of Ryukyuan music." Although he had some students for a while (nearly all young girls), the idea did not catch on and the project was doomed to failure—mostly because, I feel, he could not differentiate between the newer, powerful movements of Chinese-based Kobudo and the older, lighter movements of Te.

Te and its related weaponry, however, began to be taken much more seriously in the 1980s, under the guidance of Uehara Seikichi (of Motobu-ryu) and his former student, Higa Seitoku (at the Bugeikan), but still has not, to the best of my knowledge, been taught in any depth outside of Okinawa Prefecture except by myself. The fault, if it be a fault, has been due to its own effectiveness; in that, because so much advanced teaching was held back in the name of semi-secrecy from fear of what can be done with Te in incompetent hands, its practice was often seen, by those with a Karate background, to be ineffective.

On October 27, 1984, at the Naha City People's Hall, an unusual event took place, ushering in not only an era of understanding, but a new age of cooperation between Okinawa Prefecture and the City of Fuzhou. The event was a spectacular international demonstration of martial arts, with and without weapons, by young and old from both sides of the East China Sea. Going under the title of the China-Okinawa Martial Arts Cultural Exchange Tournament, it was a brilliant success, proven by the enthusiastic applause from the excited, packed audience, standing several persons deep in the aisles of the immense hall. The tournament was organized chiefly by the Okinawa Traditional Kobudo Preservation Society, hailing from the Bunbukan in Shuri, a model dojo with up-to-date facilities and all amenities that combines the traditional learning of Ryukyu Kobudo with conventional education. Its advent set in motion the wheels of actual "on-location" research by interested Okinawans into the history and roots of Kobudo and Karate in the Fuzhou area, as a result of which several differing newspaper articles on the complex subject were published in the *Okinawa Times* in the late 1980s, that tended, I feel, to cloud the issue even more. Given that, the articles did express a genuine desire to discover the truth about the roots through academic research and discussion into how things really were, rather than by forceful dictation as to how things should have been, or how teachers wanted them to have been, the former being a trend noticeably lacking in the past.

As for the weapons themselves? Well, they used to be handmade to order from various artisans such as the local blacksmith, for metal weapons like the *sai* metal truncheon; or by the stone bean-mill handle maker, as with the *tunfa* right-angle handle truncheon. Materials, such as locally grown tropical hardwoods, which once abounded in the Ryukyu Islands, were favored, with Yaeyama *sendangi* (sandalwood, or rosewood, from Iriomote or Ishigaki Island in Yaeyama) being the favorite. Very hard, high quality *kuroki* (ebony) was also frequently used and I once picked up a beautifully hand-fashioned ebony *bokken* (Japanese heavy wooden mock sword) for a song, but of late one would be hard-pressed to discover such a valuable item.

For the last twenty years or longer, the Kobudo weapon manufacturer Shureido has had a virtual monopoly on all Kobudo weapon manufacturing and sales in the islands. To give the owner his due, the business was built up from scratch in a tiny workshop near Sogen-ji Gate in old Tomari to meet the postwar commercial demand. Although the production is semi-automated it should not be condemned, because the quality of the Shureido weapons is excellent and to be recommended. Proof is seen in the high demand for exports all over the world and the spacious premises now used as a show-window outlet, across the busy street from the old shop.

Another Kobudo store that is not as well known as Shureido, but stocks tools and weapons of equal, if not better quality, is Okinawa Seibudo. It advertises itself as specializing in genuine Kobudo implements and also stocks kendo sports wear, sturdy Karate uniforms, and various accessories for school *budo* clubs, however, much of the merchandise is made in and imported from mainland Japan. The shop is in Matsugawa, Naha, in the enviable position of being "near the Matsugawa police box." Wherever one shops for Kobudo weaponry and wherever it is manufactured, though, it must be remembered that the tools and weapons are made in good faith for the express purpose of training and demonstration only; they are not meant to be weapons for committing violent acts.

Uehara Seikichi and Motobu-ryu

Uehara Seikichi was born in 1904 and trained in Te for over seven years under his only teacher, Motobu Choyu, until the latter's death in 1926. Two years previous to his death, Motobu Choyu had, along with some of the Karate notables of the times, such as his younger brother Motobu Choki, Goju-ryu's Miyagi Chojun, Mabuni Kenwa, and Kyan Chotoku, opened and become president of the Okinawa Tode Research Club. Under its guise, regular meetings and discussions were held at Naminoue in Naha, covering the intricacies and development of Tode, Kobudo, and Te. It fell on Uehara Seikichi to be tea boy at these meetings, but, shortly after Motobu Choyu's death, the club was disbanded and no one, except Uehara, was any the wiser as to the true depth of the Motobu family system.

Motobu Choyu's eldest son had little desire to learn the ancient family Te and, like so many of his contemporaries, found it more profitable to seek work in Wakayama Prefecture on the Japanese mainland, where he eventually settled

Uehara Seikichi.

for good, rarely, if ever, returning to his homeland. Thus Uehara Seikichi was left by fate in the enviable position of having to pass on the style, which he named Motobu-ryu in 1947. Deciding that the best way to preserve Te would be to bring it to the attention of the public and popularize it as his teacher had tried to do, he began a series of open-house demonstrations; the first being in 1964 at Kumamoto Prefecture's Okinawa Festival. Then, in 1969, he founded the Motobu-ryu Kobu-jutsu Association as an affiliated branch of the All Okinawa Karate and Kobudo Combined (or United) Association, that had been set up under the auspices of his student Higa Seitoku in 1967.

On September 22, 1974, Uehara Seikichi, along with

Higa Seitoku and his son Kiyohiko, plus Uehara's students and members of his other branch dojos, gave an important demonstration called "The First Motobu-ryu Sashiki Tournament." Although it was held at the nondescript location of the Sashiki Village elementary school gym, it went a long way to opening the doors of Te a little wider to the general public and broke through the psychological barrier of semi-secrecy that had held the style back for so long. The event was sponsored by the *Okinawa Times* and aided by one of Uehara's top students, Miyagi Takao, who worked for the newspaper. Miyagi wrote an introductory passage in the catalogue for this event which, unknowingly on his part perhaps, was probably the first published article to explain what had been until then the "mysteries" of Te. Effectively, with a few strokes of his mighty pen, he was formally annulling the unwritten law of secrecy once and for all. Translated into English, the short article reads as follows:

WHAT IS MOTOBU-RYU "TE"?
by Miyagi Takao

Motobu-ryu is the secret Te of the kings of Ryukyu that was handed down through the Motobu Udun family. It was passed on only to the eldest sons and, after the abolition of the clans, it was known only to Motobu Choyu, nicknamed Umei Anjikata. The techniques of Motobu-ryu differ from those of regular Karate katas and postures, for, to the utmost degree, the movements of the body are done with softness and opponents are thrown by using hand grappling techniques. At a casual glance, it can be mistakenly thought that there is no real technique involved, but on engagement any man, whatever his size, can be overpowered. That is to say, it is such an uncanny martial art that it is possible, by utilizing the martial strength in the hands, to achieve a submissive state without causing bodily injury to an opponent; but if more pressure is applied in the techniques, it can indeed result in a hidden death blow.

Weapons in Motobu-ryu include: *goshaku jo, nijo tanbo, uchi bo, jo, nunchaku, tonfa, kai* or *eku, nicho kama, sai, yari, naginata, katana,* and *tanto;* and besides these, any object close at hand can be used as a weapon.

The techniques of Te start with *moto-te* (original-hand), then go on to *kihon-te* (basic-hand), *tori-te* (hand-grappling), *tori-te gaeshi* (hand-grappling return), *uragaeshi* (reversal); others include: *ogami-te* (prayer-hand), *kaeshi-te* (return-hand), *karami-te* (tangled-hands), *nuki-te* (draw-hand), and *nage-te* (throw-hand), all being techniques that could be used in an actual fight. On top of these comes the deepest secret principle, known as *Anjikata no Mai no Te* (Dance Hand of the Lords). The techniques of this are truly truculent, as shown by the words in a Ryukyuan song, "Never think of just observing *Anjikata no Me Kata* (Dance Kata of the Lords), for technique compounds technique and the more the secrets come to light." In other words, the real techniques are not to be found so much in the outward form, but more in the internal dance and body movements that can manifest all the martial strength together, combining it into a mortal blow. All the punches and kicks of Motobu-ryu can be used in actual fight situations; in attack there is defense, while defense becomes attack. In any event the distinction is to place importance on technique rather than physical strength.

It can be said that, as an ancient form of Ryukyuan martial art, Motobu-ryu does indeed have real cultural value. At present the nucleus dojo is the Seidokan at Ojana, with others at Shuri (the Bugeikan), Gushikawa (the Shubukan), Goya Road (the Seidokan), and at Tetokon village, Sashiki (the Shodokan).

Following the success of the tournament at Sashiki village, the first of a well-organized and illustrated series of demonstrations entitled *Bu to Mai* (Martial Arts and Dance), was held at the smarter, more accessible central location of the Okinawa Times Hall, in Naha City, on August 20th, 1976. In the pamphlets for this and the follow-up demonstration the next year, Miyagi Takao went to great lengths to further break the secrecy code and explain his teacher's Motobu-ryu, with the ins and outs of Te, to a still largely unenlightened public. The two demonstrations were so successful that they were followed by others and are now held on an annual basis, with Uehara Seikichi taking the lead, along with Miyagi Takao and other seniors per-

Motobu-ryu Te glaive versus spear.

forming the more showy throwing and grappling stunts. Juniors usually demonstrate the simpler basics. The result has been a more general acceptance of Te in the Karate world and an awareness among the general public that such a historic art form does indeed exist, an art form that needs to be passed on and preserved for posterity.

At the present, Uehara continues to teach regularly at his modern third-floor dojo, the Seidokan in Ojana, central Okinawa. The teaching in basics is subdued, but still makes for an excellent workout with sensible stretching techniques and good, springy footwork. Besides the kata *Moto-te Sanchin,* he does not teach anything resembling Karate kata, but several of the branch dojos include these as a major part of their curricula in order, one must suppose, to appease the Karate fraternity. Weapons and Te dance forms or techniques are not taught to beginners and are kept for an exclusive group of students at the Seidokan who have demonstrated a clear ability to understand the responsibilities involved in learning such potentially dangerous techniques—the dangers being mostly in the learning process itself, should an irresponsible student decide to show off his or her physical prowess and be at the unfortunate receiving end of his or her own stupidity.

The Higa Family and the Bugeikan

Three members of Higa Seitoku's immediate family are directly involved in weapon training, Te, and Kobudo. They are, namely, Higa Seitoku himself, his son Kiyohiko, and his daughter Reiko; other family members have an indirect involvement. Having first started to learn Karate from his father Miinshiin when he was five years old in 1927, Seitoku went on to learn some basic Te techniques from the age of twelve from a teacher going by the name of Kishimoto Soko,

Higa Kiyohiko demonstrates a Te joint-locking technique.

who, in 1943, finally awarded him his teacher's license. After the Second World War, during the latter part of which he saw military service on the island of Sumatra in Indonesia, Higa Seitoku returned to Japan, where he lived on the mainland for a short while and taught his Karate and Te in Kumamoto Prefecture. There he was awarded a 7th Dan grade from the All Japan Karate Association in 1947. After returning to his homeland of Okinawa in 1950, he started to teach Te, along with Karate, in the village of Akahira in Shuri.

By 1951 he had opened his own dojo in Shuri on the

present site of the Bugeikan near the busy Gibo crossroads and, while performing the paid duties of a notary public under the U.S. Ryukyu administration, he raised his three children there. Not being totally satisfied with his knowledge of the fighting arts as it stood however, he started making visits to and learning as much as he could from many of the top teachers of the time. These included (from 1956) Chinen Masami of Yamani-ryu *bo-jutsu* fame, who like most of his contemporaries, has since died. The year 1961 saw Higa Seitoku take up serious advanced Motobu-ryu Te training and weaponry under Uehara Seikichi, forming a close teacher-student relationship that lasted many years. In the same year he founded the Okinawan Kobudo Association that by 1967 had grown and was transformed into a partnership with his All Okinawa Karate and Kobudo United Association; an umbrella group covering several styles of Karate, Te, and Kobudo that was dedicated to the individual development and recognition of each style.

To further advertise and formalize this advent, he organized, using the talents of many other teachers, a historically significant demonstration that was well sponsored by both the *Okinawa Times* newspaper and the Ryukyuan Government Cultural Preservation Society. It was held on June 11, 1967 at the Ryukyu University Sports Hall in Shuri and was appropriately entitled *Karate Kobudo no Enbu to Shiai Taikai* (Demonstration of Karate (with) Kobudo and Competition Tournament). Typically, Higa Seitoku made sure of being the self-styled centerpiece of the whole works by becoming President of the All Okinawa Karate and Kobudo United Association, cleverly listing under his presidentship such eminent names as the elderly Nakamura Heisaburo, who was minimally designated "Head of the Motobu Peninsula Area Branch," and the masterfully skillful Kojo Kafu who was merely put down as head of his own style, namely Kojo-ryu. Other representative styles (along with their respective headmasters and associations) listed in the program for the event were of course Motobu-ryu, plus Okinawa Kenpo, Isshin-ryu, Shorin-ryu (Shaolin), Shorin-ryu (Kobayashi), Goju-ryu, Matsumura Orthodox Shorin-ryu, Mabuni Kenwa Shito-ryu, Shiroma Shinpan Shito-ryu, Ryuei-ryu, Yamani-ryu, Kushin-ryu, Ryukyu Kobudo, and Kokusai Kobudo. There were also representative participants from the Ryukyu-American International Karate-do Federation and the Ryukyu University Karate-do Research Association. Interestingly enough though, some styles were even listed as such before proper recognition from their own founders.

Bugeikan (Martial Arts Hall) as a name for Higa Seitoku's dojo and his personalized martial arts system was officially adopted by him in 1968. Thus it is claimed not to be the name of his own style, but a label for his collection of various forms, fighting methods, and weaponry taken and adapted from any number of Okinawan styles.

Te and its related weaponry is taught as a mainstream element of his classes, but kept apart as a quite different entity from his Karate/Kobudo curriculum. Although the casual observer may not be able to differentiate between the two streams, a two-hour beginners' training session may start with Karate training, then lead on to Kobudo kata, and finish with vital elements of Te.

More advanced students concentrate solely on Te and its related weaponry, with much emphasis placed on fixed sparring incorporating grappling and throws, using harmless rubber knives for safety. The whole of the Bugeikan dojo floor is laid with thick straw tatami mats covered over with synthetic rubber to cushion the breakfalls.

Naturally enough, school-age children practice just the basic movements and simplified variations of standard

Karate katas taken mostly from Shorin-ryu, a term used to designate a group of Karate styles that were developed mainly in the Shuri area and originally, but confusingly, lumped together under the label Shuri-te.

Te is an art. All who practice an art form should, within reason, be free to express their own art in their own peculiar way; for without freedom of interpretation where would an art be? However, as previously touched upon, a martial art without a soul, without Zen, is a mere mechanical process, a pretty dance; a plastic rose without scent or sap and devoid of any feelings, life, or tenderness. In my experience, no other martial arts school in Okinawa that I have had the chance to train at (and I have trained at many) holds this concept more than the Bugeikan. Zen as an art is an unspoken, yet built in, part of the Bugeikan training.

Looking at the three Higa family members already mentioned, it is possible to discern three different interpretations of Te. Higa Seitoku has a characteristic style derived more from his first teachers and intuition (his *kami*) that does not emphasize the sometimes fancy footwork of Te at all. The result is that he at times may appear to be hesitant, even unsteady, in his movements—like a tottering child perhaps, or an old man on his last legs. However this illusion can often be misleading, for his body maneuvering and hand gestures are extremely to the point; in fact, he exudes an uncanny energy through them. In many ways, when in action, he is like a highly polished and well-tuned classic vintage sports car on an economy run. All is very tidy and in its proper place. No movement is wasted, no motion is ill spent.

Kiyohiko Higa, Higa Seitoku's only son, on the other hand, relies heavily on Uehara Seikichi's Motobu-ryu Te style and flashes off his unique technique, more like a finely tuned racing machine that is all out to win; probably producing the most fanciful coordinated foot and hand movements possible to mankind—and with the horsepower to go with it. This, combined with his long study of Te's distant cousin, Japanese aikido, gives his brand of Te a sharply discerning appeal, with enormously rounded movements, as when multi-dimensional circles are described within mobile spheres. In a successful attempt to recreate his own rendition of *Anjikata no Me Kata,* he will sometimes be seen at popular tournaments performing his Te while expertly foiling, yet seeming to be playing with, a football-sized metal ring held in one or both hands. Thus his Te can be a crowd-gasping display of incredibly interwoven movements and, although sometimes unreasonably criticized as being "light and fairy in his antics" by some Karate "experts," it should be taken deadly serious. The ultra-sprung crispness of his Kobudo katas is not to be scoffed at either. His shiatsu technique is in the expert category, too. Away from the dojo though, Higa Kiyohiko is a high-school mathematics teacher by profession, a recognized calligrapher, and the proud father of four talented offspring.

Comparatively speaking (if comparing someone to the best is a good thing), Seitoku Higa's daughter, Reiko, appears, at first glance, to have gained little martial value from her long-time training. She prefers to demonstrate her acute ability at performing Te using such weapons as the *nunchaku* and *tunfa* that are usually associated more with the Chinese-based Kobudo armory. Her forte is to practice with these in a set sequence, using Te movements and technology dressed up in a similar way to Kobudo katas. Although the appearance is a little sloppy, in many ways the fluidity instilled is quite sensible and at this exercise, she truly excels. No teacher could ask for a better assistant in the dojo than Higa Reiko, though, for her instruction is top class and she is always willing to give a helping hand to juniors whenever needed, especially where form is concerned. Herself a math major, she is obviously enamored of her elder brother Kiyohiko, who she justly looks up to with much due respect.

As head of the Bugeikan, Higa Seitoku is often approached by foreign nationals from such diverse countries as the U.S.A., India, France, and Australia for instruction, but is hesitant about taking them on as students. To the best of my knowledge, I am the only foreign national to have trained for any worthwhile length of time at the Bugeikan, having also become a close friend and adviser to Higa Kiyohiko's family and an English teacher to his children. According to Higa Seitoku, the Bugeikan Kobudo and Te is not *go* (hard), but relies on the *ju* (soft), having in itself defense techniques whereby a trainee should have enough leeway in controlling the aggression of a hypothetical adversary to keep him or her from harm's way. A large part of the training nowadays is dance, "to nourish the secret principles of *ki* (intrinsic energy), which includes the *ki* of Heaven and Earth in a martial arts context."

Of late a martial dance has been developed at the Bugeikan, the movements of which, for the initiated at least, can be learned within a few short days. In order to feel the *ki* circulating when doing such a "dance," however, takes a good deal more endeavor under the guidance of a masterful teacher, with constant correction. Then, to put this fully into one's martial art and become one with it, involves long and dedicated practice. "The art of Te cannot possibly be mastered in a few weeks or even years, it takes a lifetime." Since the age of sixty and reputedly due to ailing health, Higa Seitoku has admittedly done little training or teaching of the martial arts, preferring to leave this to Kiyohiko, to whom he has passed on all the major responsibilities of running the dojo. On the other hand, he has devoted much of his time to formulating, in concordance with the wishes of his wife, what he calls Seido, or, "Way of Life." This he describes as a system that, in helping to treat the body, improves the *seishin* (mind/spirit) and helps to cleanse the heart and soul.

Being a clairvoyant and self-styled *kaminchu* (spirit medium), Higa Seitoku has the air of a mystic about him, but, probably for reasons of practicality, he has tried to keep his beliefs separate from martial arts instruction. Quite frankly, students in Okinawa are usually put off by anything resembling religious ordinance—I having been one of them. The fact is that to try not to define Higa Seitoku's Seido as having religious trappings and cultish overtones, would be very difficult. Apart from the martial arts deity, Bugei no Kami, described previously, in Chapter 3, he has other "gods" *(kami)* and "goddesses" *(megami)* at his disposal, who are also his "personal spiritual guides." On the second floor above the dojo and adjacent to his family living quarters is a semi-secret room, up to which only specially favored students are invited to go and worship. The main *kami* of the pantheon of gods enshrined therein on the altar shelves of this clean and bright, incense-scented room is "U Ting O," the King of Heaven. However, other lesser ones, such as "Haha Shin," the Mother Goddess and the Japanese Shichifukujin are also displayed there, as is the phoenix, and an array of Chinese dragons. Although it is not within the realm of this work to include a summary of Higa Seitoku's multitudinous religious convictions, it should be made clear that they are part and parcel of Seido. Martial arts have been included in Seido to an extent, but students are free to choose not to participate in the religious ordinances or partake of the spiritual facets.

Likewise, pressure-point therapy (i.e., shiatsu) may be incorporated into Seido, but has not traditionally been associated with spirituality or religion. Neither, I should mention, have I ever seen Higa Seitoku giving instruction in, nor or treating anyone using the latter. As to the effectiveness of Seido, or lack of it, I cannot comment, but, it is important to note that the task of correct instruction of shiatsu at the Bugeikan is mostly in the capable hands of Miyagi Hiroshi, a senior at the dojo and long-recognized practitioner of repute on Okinawa. Shiatsu therapeutic pressure-point massage was formerly known as *anma* in Japan and is consistent with Te technique and dynamics. It is thought to have been introduced to Japan from India by Daruma in the sixth century, along with his martial arts and Zen.

The International Shiatsu Association defines shiatsu as:

> A word of Japanese origin, literally meaning finger pressure. . . The term is generally used however, to denote any therapy that incorporates pressure, touch, and manipulative techniques. Its main aims are to release tension, bring about a wholesome cure and to prevent disease. . . The treatment is used in a sensitive, compassionate manner, to release both emotional and physical stress or negative energy blocks (*yin,* or *inki*) and generally promote all-round health by improving the flow of vitality, i.e., positive, life force energy (*yang,* or *yoki*). Within a framework of inducing deep-seated relaxation, shiatsu thus aims to improve the flow of body fluids (lymph, blood, etc.), balance the hormone system, calm the nerves, encourage greater mental composure, induce the elimination of toxins (lactic acid, etc.) from the tissues, improve the function of the organs, increase stamina, and foster well-balanced relationships on a human level. Shiatsu should therefore aim to stimulate the

immune system overall, while dealing with the specific conditions of the individual, relieve painful or other symptoms and work to heal injuries, or poor health,
through self-repair. By releasing held-in tension in the
soft tissues and body organs, as well as toning the
muscle tissues, shiatsu should aim to encourage flex-
ibility of the spine and joints, as well as improving the
quality of the bones.

In martial arts on Okinawa, shiatsu has historically been
the therapeutic side of Te (which in itself is a way of health).
It is the traditional healing aspect of Zen.

Isa Shinyu and Uhuchiku Kobudo

The story behind Isa Shinyu's Uhuchiku Kobudo starts
with Kanagusuku Sanda, a gentleman of Shuri and a noted
martial artist. Having been born into a bushi family, he was
able to train in Te and various Kobudo weapons under
Matsumura Sokon, and possibly "Tode" Sakugawa, as well.
He grew up to be the father of seven children, but, sadly,
has only one remaining heir, a granddaughter by the name
of Iha Kiyo, who was born to his eldest daughter Tsuru.
Iha Kiyo (who is coincidentally related to my mother-in-
law) was born in 1904 and remembers growing up as an
orphan with her grandfather in his later years at Gibo in
Shuri. There he taught Chinese-based Kobudo in the courtyard of his home to Tsuru and a small group of eager students—while the young Kiyo looked on in wide-eyed
fascination.

According to her, Kanagusuku Sanda was actually born
"in the Chinese Year of the Bull, in about 1841," and died
unexpectedly from a cold at the age of 80, in 1921. Because of his martial prowess, he had been selected as a

young man to be a personal bodyguard and martial arts instructor to the King Sho Tai, which remained one of his official posts until about 1891. On retirement from his royal duties, Kanagusuku Sanda was appointed the first Okinawan prefectural senior chief inspector, or Uhuchiku, thence forward being known by the nickname Kinjo (a Japanization of Kanagusuku) Uhuchiku, after which Uhuchiku Kobudo is now named. The main defensive weapon carried by police officers of the day was the *sai,* and Kanagusuku Sanda soon gained a reputation as being the most knowledgeable expert in its use. Although Te-based methods of avoiding and striking in one action was his specialty, the philosophical and mental/spiritual side of martial arts training was more important to him, which he showed by imbuing such anecdotes into the minds of his faithful students as, "A true master need only attack and disarm with his mind; physical training is a stairway to this end."

Unusual for the times, Kanagusuku was not very interested in macho-male alcoholic revelry. In fact he was quite easygoing and openly psychic. Once, Kiyo recalled, how he had seen a bad omen of a woman carrying a sack of soot on her head walking passed a neighbor's house and warned the neighbor that his house was in danger of catching fire. A month later the house burned to the ground after being struck by a freak bolt of lightning. In his old age, Kanagusuku became known by the respectful nickname, Kani Usumei and was still taking on new trainees. One of these was a twenty-four-year-old young man, Kina Shosei, who at the time was an aspiring student teacher at the Shuri Teachers' Training College. It is to him that the second phase of Uhuchiku Kobudo development is credited and I was lucky to meet and interview him, for the last time, when he was in his late nineties. He was proud of his long, memorable, and healthy life, which he attributed to having a good wife (named Kameja), regular Kobudo training, moderation in diet, and refraining from the consumption of alcohol, coffee, cigarettes, or even tea. His "Christian ideals," he thought, were also an important contributory factor to his illness-free longevity.

The only surviving direct pupil of Kanagusuku, Kina told me that he was born in 1882 at the village of Shima-bukuro that, at the time, was in the Nakagusuku district, but is now incorporated into Kita-Nakagusuku Ward. Laughingly, he remembered that, being merely the second son in a family of nine brothers and sisters, he was incessantly teased by the other village children and scolded by the adults for his youthful antics. After graduating from the teachers' training college at the age of twenty-five, he became a full-time primary school teacher, but managed to continue his weapon training under Kanagusuku Sanda for a total of five years. On leaving the teaching profession at the accepted retirement age of fifty-five, Kina Shosei entered the dodgy world of local politics, becoming, after the war, a council member and parliamentary representative for Nakagusuku, in the Ryukyuan Government puppet assembly. At the same time, he started to accept trainees who wanted to learn Kobudo in general, but concentrated on teaching them Kanagusuku's favorite weapon, the *sai*.

One such trainee was the promising Kyan Shinyei, who himself took up politics during the difficult years of the American military administration. However, due to his concern for the silent majority of Okinawan country folk and because of his pro-Japanese, pro-reversion stance, he was branded, by paid C.I.A. agents, as anything from "a dangerous peace agitator" to "a red communist insurgent." Not surprisingly, he suffered for his humanitarian views, especially during the Vietnam War years when Okinawa was an indispensable U.S. Marine training ground, military supply base, and R & R facility for war-weary GIs. By the early eighties though, ten years after reversion to Japan, Kyan had finally cleared his name and shown his mettle as a democratically minded politician who sincerely cared for the welfare of his constituents. He is also famous island-wide for his powerful demonstrations of *sai* techniques and katas.

Cold reality, although important, is not always what it seems to be. The realization that reality is a fluid concept, only relevant to the space/time/situation in which it occurs, is close to discovering Zen in one's heart. Versatility is the key to true mastery of weapons and Kina Shosei made world headlines when he was to put this concept of reality to the test. It was in early April of 1945, during the first few days of the Invasion of Okinawa. Due to his respected status in the farming community, it was natural that the frightened villagers of Shimabukuro should come to Kina Shosei for guidance as to what to do about the American advance from the north. They needed protection from what they had been led to believe would mean certain rape and torture. However, rather than arm the villagers with makeshift weapons (as he had been instructed to do by the Japanese militarists), then fruitlessly attack the "enemy," Kina thought of a better idea. To have confronted the wary Americans head-on with violence would have meant certain death, so, fearful as he was, he bravely walked unarmed toward the American front line and in broken English declared himself to be an Okinawan Christian, a man of peace. The strategy worked and he was met by an expatriate interpreter who turned out to be an old pupil of his from his school teaching days. As a result of this encounter, the villagers were not harmed and were treated with extra generosity by the trusting U.S. servicemen.

Whether due to mere coincidence, a miracle, or because of the law of cause and effect, known as karma (for who can really say?), the Nakagusuku area was spared much of the destruction that tore the rest of Okinawa Island apart, during the three-month-long battle that followed the initial invasion—the battle that was to prove to be the last of World War II. Nakagusuku Castle, unlike Shuri and others, was barely scratched and still remains much as it did over five hundred years ago and, to relate a story to prove a point here, I was very fond of taking walks around the snake-infested hills of Nakagusuku in the early 1970s. Sometimes, during these escapades, I would stumble across evidence of an unexplained sudden Japanese troop withdrawal from the area.

In one place, across a gully between two enormous weather-worn, jagged coral rocks, I discovered several half-rotted, unhewn wooden poles that had, sometime in the past, been wedged across there horizontally at eye level, as if to support a protective canvas cover. Because of the number of discarded wartime Japanese medicine bottles lying scattered all around the site, I concluded that it had been a hastily evacuated Imperial Army mobile hospital unit. In several other hillside locations I found, strewn haphazardly in undisturbed circles and lying abandoned on the jungle floor, an array of cooking and eating utensils. It was as if a picnic had been left uneaten; perhaps the partakers' last meal. Many of the utensils were half buried in decayed black humus, accumulated from thirty years of fallen jungle vegetation. A strange memorial, I thought, to those young Japanese soldiers who had retreated farther south to fight their enemy at the suicide cliffs of Mabuni, never to return in body to the haven of their home villages, towns, and islands.

The formulation of Kanagusuku's Kobudo into a style

and the naming of it as "Uhuchiku Kobudo," is the responsibility of another of Kina Shosei's trainees, a Buddhist priest by the name of Isa Shinyu. When I first met him at his quaint Kannon-do Temple in Futenma, Central Okinawa, I was in the repository annex building searching among the layers of dark, ghostly shelves stacked with dusty funerary jars, trying to locate the potted ashes and family altar of Kanagusuku Sanda—Iha Kiyo told me she had left them there for safekeeping. As I had planned, a black-robed Isa Shinyu confronted me, asking politely what on earth a red-bearded foreigner was doing snooping around his temple with a camera. After explaining my sincerity in the matter, he showed me what I had been looking for and we sat on a convenient bench to have a pleasant impromptu discussion. I knew that Kanagusuku was there listening to us.

Isa Shinyu informed me that he was born in 1943, in a village that is no more, but used to be where a part of the sprawling American Kadena Air Base is now located. He started to learn Karate after the war, at the age of three, from his grandfather. When older he trained in Kobudo under Kina Shosei, but has also studied under Uehara Seikichi of Motobu-ryu, as well as a teacher called Tokashiki Saburo who was already deceased. A historian in his own right, Isa believes that many of the Okinawan styles originated a full 1,600 years ago, at the Shaolin Temple in Northern China, and seemed to support the theory that the monks there trained in weapons to protect themselves from frequent attacks by bandit hordes. He confirmed that, on Okinawa, after the Satsuma invasion, weapon training, although forbidden, was passed down in samurai families from father to son in secrecy, also explaining that he believed the training was done at inaccessible places between dusk and dawn, away from the eyes and ears of the informers. Indeed, all such training was traditionally performed in the cool of the evening anyway to avoid the harmful sun's rays. Of necessity too, training was done in open spaces, such as gardens, festival sites, and sacred groves, that were often away from the main village and surrounded by thick clumps of protected evergreen trees and bushes.

Some of Kina's ideas were a bit too much to swallow, though, as when he insisted that all Kobudo weapons, apart from the *sai,* had been developed by Okinawans from their utensils—theories that are quite popular and seemingly plausible until the facts are examined. On my visiting his Shudokan (a comparatively small wooden dojo) some time later, Isa proudly showed me his antique Okinawan weapon collection that is unmatched anywhere else on the island. At the time I noted his Kobudo was powerfully impressive and well controlled; on reflection, it was an accurate statement. As for Isa's priestly activities, he explained that he had studied Buddhism at the Somotosan Denpo Monastery in Kyoto, which is of the Shingon sect, and on graduating became one of the directors of the Futenma Kannon-do, which is a family concern. In Japan in general, and more so in Okinawa, the role of a Buddhist priest is to be concerned mostly with ceremonial ritual. Thus a priest is thought of as being a paid profession and is not expected to live a contemplative way of life.

Isa conforms to the social norm in this respect and his role as a Kobudo teacher is kept separate from his work. Even then, he holds the theory that Daoist and Buddhist meditative practices were incorporated into the martial art systems of Okinawa to become part of the techniques; not vice-versa. He recognizes the close relationship between physical therapy and weapons training, stating that "an illness-free and strong physique with an alert mind, free from tensions and stress, is the aim of martial arts practice." To him, therefore, the influence of religion (Buddhism) improved primitive fighting systems, along with medicine, early psychology, and the understanding of physiology. "Primitive men with crude weapons," he surmised, "became civilized through adopting meditative practices and the influence of organized religion."

Akamine Eisuke's Ryukyu Kobudo

In order to trace the history of Akamine Eisuke's Ryukyu Kobudo, one has to first journey back to the time of Yabiku Moden (1882–c.1945), an Okinawan who founded the Ryukyu Kobu-jutsu Research Association (Ryukyu Kobu-jutsu Kenkyukai) in about 1911 and who is usually credited with having first introduced Okinawan Kobudo to the Japanese mainland. One of his teachers had been Chinen Sanda, who had learned Kobudo from his own father, Chinen Pechin, who in turn had trained under Sakugawa Satunushi, a student of the Chinese named Kusanku. Two of Yabiku's other teachers were Tawata Pechin (also nicknamed, Tawata nu Meigantu) and Kanagusuku Sanda, who had both been students of Matsumura Sokon. The Ryukyu Kobu-jutsu Research Association lasted until Yabiku's death, which is thought to have been sometime during the end of the Second World War.

After that, a top disciple of his, Taira Shinken (c.1897–1970), who had been teaching Kobudo on Okinawa since about 1940, took over teaching responsibilities and founded the Society for the Promotion and Preservation of Ryukyuan Kobudo (Ryukyu Kobudo Hozon Shinkokai), which he presided over until his death at the age of seventy-three. One of his last wishes was that his favorite trusted student, Akamine Eisuke, succeed him. This Akamine agreed to do and, keeping Taira's association under the original title, named the style Ryukyu Kobudo when he opened his own dojo, the Shinbukan, in 1971. Perhaps the

Yabiku Moden.

Taira Shinken wearing protective training equipment.

Akamine Eisuke wielding a staff.

most helpful and open of all the Kobudo teachers I have interviewed or trained under, Akamine is obviously proud of the cultural heritage he has inherited and only too pleased to show it off, which he does in a demonstrative, matter-of-fact way, with no holds barred.

He was born at Kakazu, southern Okinawa, on May Day in 1925 and, from 1948, before becoming a disciple of Taira Shinken in 1959, he trained in the staff *(bo-jutsu)* under two of Chinen Sanda's students, namely Higa Sei-ichiro and Kisuke. By 1965, he had received permission from Taira Shinken to teach Kobudo and, since establishing his own dojo, he has been able to open many branch clubs of Ryukyu Kobudo. These have flourished and are to be found as far and wide apart as the Japanese mainland and the United States of America.

At the Shinbukan, Akamine teaches the use of twelve different Kobudo weapons, including the *tekko*, or iron fist, an unusual piece of armory that would no doubt come under the generic, not-so-genteel, term "knuckle-duster" in the English vernacular. As the major part of Ryukyu Kobudo, he also preserves for posterity's use and enjoyment thirteen staff katas, eight *sai* katas, two *tunfa* katas, and one kata each respectively of *nunchaku, kai,* and *kama*. There are also some regular Karate katas that Taira Shinken learned from Funakoshi Gichin and passed on to Akamine. As far as the development of Kobudo on Okinawa goes, Akamine sees it more in the simplistic light of most Naha townspeople who, of necessity, do not generally claim *shizoku* ancestry and often know nothing about Te, its development, or its techniques. Thus, he feels that, after the subjugation by Satsuma and the subsequent enforcement of the weapon edicts, gentlemen of Shuri started to train defensively with farm and household implements, eventually forsaking the banned bladed weapons.

With the gradual introduction of Shaolin-based forms and techniques from China over the last two hundred years or so, he believed that Kobu-jutsu, a new style of weapon-based self-defense, gradually developed among the towns-people of Shuri and later Naha. This eventually changed from "traditional Kobu-jutsu" into the modern Kobudo that is preserved today and epitomized by Ryukyu Kobu-do. Most of the Kobudo katas that are extant in Okinawa, he feels, were created by Okinawans, in the nineteenth and early twentieth centuries, from Chinese prototype move-ments and are more for show, rather than self-defense. Of-fensive and defensive techniques against the rounded, slicing movements of curved bladed weapons, like the sword and glaive, are, as in most Karate styles, rarely included as part of Kobudo practice outside of the dojos where Te-based weaponry is taught, namely, Uehara Seikichi's Seidokan and Higa Seitoku's Bugeikan.

An interesting development to come out of Ryukyu Kobudo is the idea that sport staff fighting, like sport Kara-te, can be enjoyable and yet remain safe for the battling adherents. The concept actually goes back a long way and, in this respect, Taira Shinken tried out the use of several types of "battle dress" to act as body protectors. They had to be strong enough to resist the full force of a staff, flexible enough so as not to impede maneuverability, and light enough not to hinder speed. A photograph taken in 1934 shows him dressed up in a patchwork of various bits and pieces of body armor, including boxing gloves, rounded metal shoulder pads and a lace-up chest protector; pre-sumably this being reinforced with bamboo canes. Aka-mine Eisuke found that the breastplate, helmet and gloves of ordinary sport kendo (Japanese fencing) body armor, were an adequate compromise for sport staff fighting, as long as the strikes were even more restricted than those used in kendo. Such limitations meant, for example, that the unprotected legs and back could not be struck, nor could the top of the head. It ruled out the use of forward lunge strikes to the face or throat as well, an essential precaution in case the staff broke and the resulting jagged point pierced through the oblong slits in the wire face mask, penetrating the opponent's face or eyes. Also, a sudden thrust to the forehead could jerk the head backwards suddenly, causing a whiplash-type injury.

Because of the amount of weapon breakage that occurred while fighting with ordinary machine-turned wooden staffs and the very real dangers the resulting knife-like edges presented, developing a suitable staff for sport bouts has remained a constant and nagging problem. Originally, slatted bamboo staffs, that looked like two kendo *shinai* (slatted bamboo practice swords) joined together at their handles, were experimented with, but found to be unsuitable because the springiness made them inadequate for blocking—an essential part of Kobudo sparring. By 1976, when the first official sport staff competition bout was held under the auspices of Ryukyu Kobudo, no one had come up with a better solution to the problem, so ordinary staffs were used. Most of these locally manufactured weapons, being meant for kata practice, were not strong enough for the rigors of competition and subsequently broke during the course of events.

For the follow-up competition, held the following year in 1977 at the Bunbukan dojo in Shuri (which was overseen by, among others, Akamine Eisuke, Nakama Chozo, Higa Yuchoku, and myself) a completely new type of staff was tried out. This was a green-colored, six-foot, hollow fiberglass pole with a rubber cap stuck on each end; but one wonders if these had not been borrowed from some Okinawan housewife's washing line, as the same poles are

Staff sparring at the Bunbukan in 1977.

standard equipment all over Japan for hanging out heavy-duty washing, or airing futon bedding on sunny days. Small trucks and other vehicles loaded with such washing poles and paraphanalia, that were traditionally made of bamboo, ply the streets of Naha with blaring loudspeakers, monotonously advertising their wares. Although these low-tech poles were really a little too light in weight for sport staff fighting, they were springy enough to absorb some harder blows without physically damaging the person on the receiving end (or the attacker's hands) and not too springy to prevent blocking.

In a way, the fiberglass pseudo-staffs were a good idea and the competition matches they were fought over looked very impressive. The problem was that, whenever full force was applied to a really skillful strike or block, the staffs would embarrassingly crumple and finish up with broken ends flopping around in limp protest to their harsh treatment. Brutal punishment indeed, for which poles intended for use on Japanese laundry lines had not been designed. The breakage rate of these fiberglass poles, that day in 1977, was so high that the entire stock was soon depleted and it was back to basics, with the expensive, regular training staffs at the dojo hurriedly drafted into service. Being stronger and a little more durable than their fiberglass substitutes, it was thought, these at first appeared to fare well, but were shown to be too brittle under the constant violent stress and strain of mock combat. So, unfortunately, they did not last long either before they started snapping into bits and pieces, with chunks of broken ends flying dangerously across the dojo into the spectators (including myself) watching from the sides—luckily, though, none of the onlookers was hurt.

Much has been done since then to find the right ingredients for successful sport staff matches. This includes experiments with heavier carbon-fiber staffs that need to be thickly padded at both ends with cumbersome, vinyl-wrapped, spongy wadding, which tends to cause too much air resistance and drastically slows down the strike and block sequences, with unsatisfactory results. None of these attempts has therefore come near to combining reality with safety in a truly effective manner that closely emulates combat situations. Thus practical research to develop sensible equipment with the appropriate rules for sport staff fighting continues.

Miyagi Masakazu and Honshin-ryu

Perhaps Miyagi Masakazu, founder of the Honshin-ryu Karate and Kobudo Preservation Society (Honshin-ryu

Miyagi Masakazu.

Karate Kobudo Hozon Kai), that is based on the Motobu
Peninsula, has the nearest solution to the above problem—
albeit a traditional one. That is, in the guise of the old *kumi*
weapon katas or dances. These involve two or more participants working in unison together, as a team, in a set sequence of coordinated movements that alternately parallel
and then clash with each other in fairly realistic strike and
block routines. As practiced in the dojo, the *kumi* katas

become self-defense fighting sequences for health and spiritual development, whereas at festivals, with the accompaniment of loud, crashing gongs and other noisy musical instruments, the same set of movements come over as harsh, vibrant martial-arts based *kumi* dances. There is actually little differentiation between the two apart from the intent in the minds of the practitioners at the time of the performance, as to whether they consider the forms to be an expression of martial valor or an expressive weapon dance. Technique is indistinguishable, intent is the deciding factor.

Festivals with such displays of past martial heritage are popular, lively events in many villages on the Motobu Peninsula; a rocky, mountainous area, with deep valleys and orange groves to which many Shuri families emigrated after the slackening of restrictions on their movements in the early seventeen hundreds. For motives known only to themselves, but certainly not in an attempt to overthrow the legitimate Ryukyuan government or Satsuma, a few of the male inhabitants traveled from the Motobu Peninsula to Fuzhou for periods of up to about ten years, in the seventeen and eighteen hundreds, for the purpose of learning Chinese Shaolin-based weaponry at the Shaolin Temple there, before returning to their farms in Motobu. A theory that remnants of the defeated Ryukyuan army, who miraculously escaped the Satsuma slaughter in 1609, somehow made their way to China where they learned Kobudo at the Fuzhou Shaolin Temple is flawed in that it is generally believed that the "temple," although probably a terrorist base set up to oust the unpopular Manchu Qing rulers, was not founded until the late eighteenth century.

A quiet, unassuming man by nature and a dentist by profession, Miyagi Masakazu, who was born in 1921, teaches his Honshin-ryu Kobudo and Karate at his spacious, utilitarian, concrete dojo, the Motobu Kan, which is situated in the quaint Motobu fishing-port town of Toguchi. Beginning his Karate training at Koza (now Okinawa City) under Uechi Kanyei of Uechi-ryu, he went on to learn Chinese-based Kobudo, along with Karate, from a number of teachers who included the *sai* expert and noted politician, Kyan Shinyei and a teacher from Motobu called Nakamura Heisaburo (c.1894–1975), a former headmaster of Toguchi High School. Nakamura had been a Kobudo and Karate student of Kuniyoshi Shinkichi, who had learned his skills from Sakiyama Kitoku—he who had journeyed to China and trained with Nakaima Norisato in Ru Ru Ko's dojo at Fuzhou. In turn, Kuniyoshi Shinkichi, who before the war ran a dojo at Miyazato village near Toguchi, influenced (among others) the Kobudo of Nakamura Shigeru (c. 1892–1969), founder of the style he named Okinawa Kenpo in the 1950s. The usual Kobudo weapons, *bo, sai, tonfa,* and *kama,* are taught by Miyagi, as part of Honshin-ryu, along with their appropriate katas.

Treated as living organisms with minds of their own, as the phraseology surrounding them suggests, the origins of these katas are not always traceable, but obviously contain techniques going back to the Chinese originals. These include some katas Miyagi has learned, and thus "collected," from various villages and towns on the Motobu Peninsula, where they still survive in festivals, yet, being on the endangered list, always face the possibility of becoming extinct. Of particular value to Miyagi are those *kumi* katas among his collection that were created by Kuniyoshi Shinkichi for festival use. In this respect, the Honshin-ryu Karate and Kobudo Preservation Society has an important role to play in preserving and passing on these intangible cultural assets for the enjoyment of future generations, just as a National Trust would restore, maintain, and pass on for posterity tangible assets such as important historical buildings. Nowadays the need for such preservation societies is all the greater because, whereas before the Second World War all fit and healthy children (including robust girls) were either goaded or forced to learn and perform the katas for the village festivals by the militarily inspired youth group leaders, the interest nowadays, with the lack of enforcement, has naturally waned.

The result is that most men (and some women) who were born in the 1920s and 1930s can evidently wield a staff effectively, while the majority of those born in postwar generations cannot; a situation that from the traditionalists' point of view is sometimes seen to represent social decay or decadence. This is despite the fact that the prewar youth groups were unknowingly preparing their members for a disastrous, suicidal battle that was beyond their innocent comprehension. Under the constant duress and indoctrinatory pressures, members of these youth groups frequently grouped together and, for the most minimal of excuses, resorted to vigilante-type beatings using their sticks and staffs.

In the years before the war, when outward expressions of affection were considered wrong by the military and came to be regarded as morally unacceptable throughout society in general, it was even difficult for a boy to date a girl from another village. If such an affair was uncovered, the offending youth would, if trapped and caught, be subjected to a good beating from the youth group members of the girl's village.

These were not isolated incidents by any means and mob rule was certainly not confined solely to the Motobu area alone, as is illustrated by the number of romanticized stories one hears about those rough and ready times; one example being related by my elderly mother-in-law, who was

born and bred in Shuri. She had an uncle, nicknamed Irebuji no Oji (Uncle Irebuji), who was the son of a Shuri
nobleman. In his early fifties, Irebuji no Oji found himself
reduced in social status (like many of his peers), having to
drive a horse and cart for a living. Much of the work con-
sisted of hauling off-loaded cargo from the docks to warehouses and business premises in Naha whenever a ship
came in. All was going well and Irebuji no Oji had been
earning a reasonable livelihood until the locals from Kaki-
nohana District in Naha, who had traditionally held the
license for hauler work by right of birth, decided to nip his
activities in the bud by bribing the policeman at the wharf
gates to refuse him entry. Angered by this and not taking
"no" for an answer, Irebuji no Oji forced his way onto the
wharf and duly proceeded to upturn all the other carts with
his bare hands—goods and all. From then on he had a free
pass of entry, but there was much unexpressed contention
about the result of the incident and even the police were
afraid to confront Irebuji no Oji head on.

Consequently, they mounted a disinformation campaign,
perpetrating a myth that he was an uncontrollable demonic beast, a fearful giant who was wont to run amok. Ru-
mors spread and multiplied until he was ambushed on the
approach road to Shuri one evening, by between ten and
fifteen well-meaning members of the Ishimine Village youth
group, who were all armed with sturdy staffs made from
freshly cut hardwood saplings. Warding them off with Te
strategies that had been passed down through his family
was no difficult task for him, until one of the youths produced a knife and attempted to use it. More urgent tactics
were needed, so Irebuji no Oji kicked this attacker in the
ribs, inflicting a wound that later turned gangrenous and
needed two weeks' hospital treatment. Exhausted and covered in blood after the fight, Irebuji no Oji was himself

transported to hospital, ironically in his own cart, but found to have no injuries at all. However, seeking retaliation, the police arrested him and summarily beat him half to death with their truncheons and in so doing broke his left collar bone. He treated this wound himself, but he retained the scar of anger over the unfortunate ugly experience for the rest of his life. Becoming a disorderly alcoholic, he could, incidentally, only be pacified by the kind and gentle, calming words of my mother-in-law's husband.

This was an era when all young men and some ladies could skillfully cut and make their own staffs; one of which is a tangible cultural asset, proudly preserved in the hands of Miyagi. Typical of the pre-war era, it is a jet-black six-footer, expertly crafted from the *shin,* or heart (the central core) of a young ebony tree. Tragically, though, such memorabilia, like most weapons, tend to bear ominous memories and the last recorded episode of such Okinawan hand-held weaponry being used en masse against an enemy force was not so long ago, for it would seem that the youth group Kobudo training had been quite effective in its scope. Sometimes, American servicemen fighting on the front lines, during the Battle of Okinawa, were surprised to witness suicide attacks by villagers and other Okinawan civilians armed with sticks, spears, or glaives. Some of these weapons are preserved at the Mabuni War Museum, near the suicide cliffs on Southern Okinawa Island and from their superior quality appear to have been valuable heirlooms, but others are noted as merely having been improvised, thick bamboo canes with sliced-off sharpened tips.

In the meticulously detailed book *Okinawa: The Last Battle* (pp. 177–80), the authors clearly record an incident that happened on Iejima, the island that looms like a gargantuan battleship off the Motobu coast. It was during the night of April 20, 1945, while U.S. troops in Second Battalion of the 307th were dug in along the hard-fought, strategic defensive lines around Government House Hill, on what they aptly labeled "Bloody Ridge." Small groups of Japanese "soldiers" had been unsuccessfully probing the American lines in the dark, trying to discover a weak point, when, at 0530 hours, after an hour-long mortar barrage by the Japanese, between three and four hundred of them stormed through their own mortar fire, into the American positions. An extremely intense and costly hour-long struggle at close quarters ensued, until things got so bad that "the U.S. battalion commander, staff officers, clerks, cooks, and drivers" were drawn into the immediate action. The Americans held on to the position, but many of their number were killed, along with all those in the attacking Japanese suicide mission. "Among them," the American narrative unemotionally records in a single icy sentence, "were women armed with spears."

Matayoshi Shinpo's Kobudo

If Miyagi Masakazu, in his peaceful, laid-back Motobu backwater, unknowingly echoes (but in no way projects) the romanticized preservation of the end of a destructive and brutal era that is to many best forgotten, Matayoshi Shinpo represents very real dynamic progression forward toward a better world of mutual cooperation. Carrying on from Matayoshi Shinko, his adventurer father who introduced Matayoshi-type Kobudo from China in 1915, Matayoshi Shinpo has continued to popularize and develop the art. He has helped in a big way to make it widely known across the planet as a healthy, safe, and creative activity for those of all ages, shapes, sizes, and backgrounds.

Before first traveling to China, at the age of about twenty-three, Matayoshi Shinko, being of Shuri ancestry, had

Matayoshi Shinko.

managed to learn the use of several Kobudo weapons, including the staff, *sai,* and *kama,* from a teacher nicknamed
Gushikawa Tiragwa, who lived near Chatan, his home town
in Central Okinawa. He had also learned the *nunchaku* and
tunfa there, from a teacher called Ire.

During that notable trip to north China, the Manchuri-
an mounted bandit gang with which he had he had somehow gotten involved taught Matayoshi Shinko the use of
the lasso and the bow and arrow, as well as knife-throwing
techniques—all accomplished on horseback.

On his return to Japan, Matayoshi Shinko gave a Kobudo demonstration at Tokyo in 1915, in conjunction with
Funakoshi Gichin, the founder there of Shotokan Karate.
Later, he gave another demonstration with Miyagi Chojun
in front of the young Crown Prince Hirohito during the
royal's well-publicized visit to Okinawa in 1921. The second visit to China, to Fuzhou and Shanghai, saw Matayoshi Shinko learning the *suruchin* (ball and chain) and

Matayoshi Shinpo.

other weaponry, together with some forms of Chinese Boxing and their related medicinal practices.

Matayoshi Shinpo, who was born in 1922, had started his martial arts training in Karate and Bo-jutsu at the age of eight under Kyan Chotoku, an influential teacher of the prewar era. When reunited with his estranged father, on the latter's return from his second Chinese adventure in 1934, the young Shinpo began to train in Tode and Kobudo under him and, in 1935, learned Chinese White Crane Boxing from Gokenki, the Chinese tea importer who had taken up residence in Naha. After his father's premature death at the age of 59, in 1947, Matayoshi Shinpo succeeded him, but had actually already been teaching Kobudo commercially in Kawasaki on the Japanese mainland, from 1945 onwards. In 1960, on his return to Okinawa, Matayoshi taught his "Ryukyuan Kobudo" in Naha City at the Shodokan dojo that was run by the noted Goju-ryu Karate teacher Higa Seiko (1898-1966), founder in 1958 of the International Karate and Kobudo Federation (Kokusai Karate Kobudo Renmei), a group that sought to combine the best elements of Karate and Kobudo.

In 1970, Matayoshi founded and presided over what he originally titled the Ryukyuan Kobudo Federation (Ryukyu Kobudo Renmei), but two years later, due in part to its similarity in name to Akamine Eisuke's Ryukyu Kobudo, he changed the name to the All Okinawa Kobudo Federation: Incorporated Body (Shadan Hojin: Zen Okinawa Kobudo Renmei). This is an independent association dedicated to the furtherance of Kobudo as a cultural asset on a global basis. Official-sounding names apart, however, the style is widely known on Okinawa as simply "Matayoshi Kobudo" and now has a large student body in various Japanese prefectures, the U.S.A., Germany, Spain, and other countries including France, where it is under the auspices of the capable Okinawan teacher Chinen Kenyu.

At Matayoshi's neat and tidy dojo near Naha, the Kodokan (Hall of the Enlightened Way), which he named in honor of his father, Shinko, he gives instruction in an array of thirteen weapons, which include several lengths of staff, the *sai* and *nunchaku kun,* etc. with an interesting agricultural tool, the *kuwa,* a heavy bladed Okinawan hoe. He has four main staff katas and one kata for the *kai.* Along with these, he teaches *suruchin, tinbei* (a sharp implement and shield), and *nuntei,* (mounted *sai*) techniques, etc., that his father learned in China. Karate (Tode) and Chinese Boxing do not comprise part of his instruction, but now and again he will demonstrate his White Crane Boxing to enthralled audiences. A sincere and, by Okinawan standards, hard taskmaster, the practical side of his father's teaching shines through and differentiates Matayoshi Kobudo from just being a collection of aesthetically attractive weapon katas and dances. Such practicalities give any style, be it Te or Kobudo, that edge of authenticity that adds a certain flair of magical fascination to a martial art; a spark of life, an infusion of zest and an intuitive understanding of Zen.

Kobudo therefore is Zen in action and Zen is a reaction to Kobudo; the result of proper training with the right psychology. The two are inextricably interlinked, entwined as it were in a cosmic interactive "dance," like the proverbial serpent eternally twisting around the Tree of Life. A dance that is not so much an outward form as an inward expression of the soul, the positive aspects of all that is human, emanating life from within. Inanimate weapons do not kill of their own accord, for it is the personality behind the wielder of the weapon that decides its use. Weapons can also be used as a prop for an outwardly expressive dance routine, but this peaceful exercise is no more the raison d'être behind Kobudo than is the war-like use of weapons for harming people. Yet as harmless and entertaining as a mere weapons dance is, such does not bear the spark, the spiritual fire, as when Zen enters the equation. The cosmic "dance" is not a dance as such but Zen in motion, turning the wheels of time and fueling the fires of transformation; that progressive element in man's universe that propels him forward to an individual and collective enlightenment. Far from being destructive, Kobudo weapons practice is a means of attaining this enlightenment, this Zen, this Way, this Truth, this Life.

Bibliography

Appleman, Roy E., James M. Burns, Russell A. Gugeler, John Stevens. *Okinawa: The Last Battle.* Tokyo: Charles E. Tuttle Co., 1960.

Bishop, Mark. *Okinawan Karate, Teachers, Styles and Secret Techniques.* London: A & C Black, 1989.

Draeger, Donn F. and Robert W. Smith. *Asian Fighting Arts.* Tokyo: Kodansha International Ltd., 1969.

Frank, Benis M. *Okinawa: Touchstone to Victory.* U.S.A.: MacDonald & Co. Ltd., 1969.

Hanayama, Shinsho and D. Litt. *A History of Japanese Buddhism.* Tokyo: Bukkyo Dendo Kyokai, 1960.

Haring, Douglas G. *Okinawan Customs, Yesterday and Today.* Tokyo: Charles E. Tuttle Co., 1969.

Kerr, George H. *Okinawa, The History of an Island People.* Tokyo: Charles E. Tuttle Co., 1958.

McFairland, Neill H. *Daruma: The Founder of Zen in Japanese Art and Popular Culture.* Tokyo: Kodansha International, 1987.

Miyazato, Eiichi. *Okinawa Goju-ryu Karate-do.* Tokyo: Jitsugyo no Sekai Sha, 1978.

Murakami, Katsumi. *Karate-do to Ryukyu Kobudo.* Tokyo: Seibido Sports Library, 1977.

Nagamine, Shoshin. *Okinawa no Karate-do: Rekishi to Densetsu o Mamoru.* Tokyo: Shinjinbutsu Oraisha, 1975

Nagamine, Shoshin. *The Essence of Okinawan Karate-do.* Tokyo: Charles E. Tuttle Co., 1976.

Ono, Keihan. *Kenpu Shukuya: Dai Ichi Bu.* Tokyo: Nihon Taido Kyokai, 1972.

Oechsle, Rob. *Aoi Me ga Mita Dai Ryukyu: Great Ryukyu Discovered—19th Century Ryukyu in Western Art and Illustration.* Okinawa: Nirai-sha, 1987.

Reischauer, August Karl. *The Nature and Truth of the Great Religions.* Tokyo: Charles E. Tuttle Co., 1966.

Robinson, James. *Okinawa, A People and Their Gods.* Tokyo: Charles E. Tuttle Co., 1969.

Smith, Robert W. *Secrets of Shaolin Temple Boxing.* Tokyo: Charles E. Tuttle Co., 1964.

Smith, Robert W. *Pa-kua: Chinese Boxing for Fitness and Self-Defense.* Tokyo: Kodansha International Ltd., 1967.

Smith, Robert W. *Hsing-i, Chinese Mind-Body Boxing.* Tokyo: Kodansha International Ltd., 1974.

Smith, Robert W. *Chinese Boxing: Masters and Methods.* Tokyo: Kodansha International Ltd., 1974.

Taira, Shinken. *Ryukyu Kobudo Taikan: Hozon Ryukyu Kobudo Shinkokai,* Okinawa: published privately, 1964.

Uechi, Kanyei. *Seisetsu Okinawa Karate-do: Sono Rekishi to Giho.* Okinawa: published privately, 1978.

Yamanouchi, Seihin. *Dance of Ryukyu and Self-Defense Dances.* Tokyo: published privately, 1963.

Glossary-Index

175